Crown Jewels

Prince Michael of Greece

Crown Jewels

Crescent Books
New York

For their valuable help in my research I wish to thank the
following people: Mr Hans Nadelhofer, Mr Francois
Curiel and Mrs Ferenzy (Christie's New York), Mr John
Bloch (Sotheby's New York), Mr Laurence Krashes
(Harry Winston, New York), and Mr William Walker
and the staff of the library of the Metropolitan Museum,
New York.

I also wish to thank the following private collectors
for their kind permission to reproduce objects in their
possession: Monseigneur le Comte de Paris, His Imperial
and Royal Highness Prince Louis Ferdinand of Prussia,
and His Royal Highness Prince Giovanni of Bourbon
Siciles.

Frontispiece **Imperial Eagle.** This jewel, in gold and
enamel and set with a beautiful garnet, was nicknamed 'the
Chimera' and was part of Louis XIV's collection.

Crown Jewels of Europe © 1983 Alexandria Press
History Unlimited Inc.
This book was designed and produced by Alexandria Press
in collaboration with John Calmann & King Ltd, London

This 1986 edition published by
Crescent Books, distributed by Crown
Publishers, Inc.

First published in Great Britain in 1983
Designer: Richard Foenander
Printed in Singapore

Library of Congress Cataloging in Publication Data

Michael, Prince of Greece, 1939–
    Crown jewels

    Reprint. Originally published: New York : Harper &
Row, c1983.
    Includes index.
    1. Crown jewels – Europe – History. 2. Regalia
(Insignia) – Europe – History. 3. Europe – Kings and
rulers – History. I. Title.
CR4480.M5   1986   739.27′094   85-28032
ISBN 0-517-48934-1

h g f e d c b a

Contents

Introduction

On Christmas Day 800, Charlemagne, on a visit to Rome, decided to go and pray at the tomb of the Apostle Peter. Charlemagne, King of the Franks, was the era's leading figure. Emerging from the barbaric chaos of the High Middle Ages, he was the first to impose some order and unity on the Continent. The venerably bearded ruler stopped neither at massacre nor even at genocide to achieve his goals – an attitude that had enabled him to gather under his sovereignty what are now France, Germany, the Benelux countries and northern Italy. He had on several occasions come to the rescue of the Pope, who as a result was deeply in his debt.

In order to perform his devotions to St Peter, Charlemagne politely exchanged his Frankish costume for the Roman tunic and cloak. One may imagine he was impressed when he entered the immense basilica of St Peter, built by the Emperor Constantine the Great. One may imagine he marvelled at the forest of columns separating the five naves, at the multicoloured marble, the glittering mosaics, the high Grecian ceilings. He knelt before the High Altar and sank into lengthy prayers. Some minutes later the Pope tiptoed up behind him and, without warning, jammed a crown on his head. The forewarned audience roared: 'To Charles August, crowned by God, Great and Peaceful Emperor of the Romans, long life and victory ...'.

The Pope had paid his debt to Charlemagne. The latter put on a great show of surprise, and swore that he had been made emperor without his knowledge or consent. Furthermore he grumbled that he had never wanted the honour, and for several years refused to wear his new title. We may well doubt his sincerity and attribute the sulking to his prodigious craftiness, for the magic dignity of Roman Emperor could not fail to flatter the ambition of a barbarian chieftain. But was it a legitimate dignity? There was after all another Roman Empire, this one authentic, ruled by the Byzantines, the legitimate heirs to Imperial Rome. It was specifically to free himself from the temporary tutelage of Byzantium that the Pope invented a new Roman Empire in the person of Charlemagne. The Byzantine Empire was ruled at the time by a woman, Empress Irene, who, though renowned for her piety, was entirely ruthless. Some evidence of this is furnished by the story that she had her son's eyes gouged out in order to rule in his place. Confronted with

2 Reliquary Bust of Charlemagne wearing a crown. The reliquary bust in gilded silver and enamel of the first Emperor of the West was commissioned in the fifteenth century by his successor, Emperor Charles IV of Luxembourg. The crown, which is in gold, precious stones and cameos, dates from the fourteenth century and was probably that of Richard of Cornwall (second son of King John of England), who had been briefly elected titular king of the Holy Roman Empire.

3 Talisman of Charlemagne. In the year 1000, for the thousandth anniversary of the birth of Christ, Emperor Otto III had Charlemagne's tomb at Aix-la-Chapelle (Aachen) opened. The great Emperor was found sitting on his marble throne, perfectly preserved, his legendary white beard spread across his chest. Otto III removed from the neck of his predecessor a talisman, two cabochon sapphires containing a relic of the True Cross set in gold and precious stones. It remained in the treasure-house until 1804, when the chapter of the cathedral presented it to Empress Josephine for her coronation. Eventually it was inherited by the wife of Napoleon III, Empress Eugénie. After the fall of the Second Empire in 1870 she took it with her into exile in England. When the Germans bombed the Cathedral of Reims in the First World War, the former Empress, overwhelmed by such an act of vandalism, returned the Talisman of Charlemagne to the cathedral, where it remains.

Charlemagne's usurpation, she conceived the simple but amazing plan of marrying him. A palace revolution overthrew her before the wedding of wise emperor and pious empress could take place.

Legitimate or not, prepared or not, Charlemagne's coronation can be called the ancestor of all European coronations. There have been three crowns of Charlemagne, two swords and one sceptre; none of these objects was used at his coronation, for none of them was yet in existence. Nothing is known of Charlemagne's crown, variously described as 'Diadem of Caesar', 'ring of gold' or 'precious crown', but it was the mother of all the crowns of Europe.

The Empire of the West, launched for Charlemagne, eventually grew into the Holy Roman Empire, which lasted under various forms for ten centuries until Napoleon abolished it with a flick of his pen in 1806. Naturally these centuries saw the emergence of instruments of imperial coronation.

First came what is known as the 'Crown of Charlemagne', the most majestic of all crowns, fashioned in the tenth and eleventh centuries. It is the epitome of the mystical symbolism so dearly loved by the Middle Ages. The octagonal shape, unique in European crowns, recalls the walls of Rome, the Ramparts of Heaven, the dignity of Emperor; the number eight is also linked to perfection and eternal life. The placing of the gems on the sides symbolizes the Revelation of St John the Evangelist and imitates the breast-plate of the High Priest of Israel. The magic with which the Middle Ages imbued precious stones is indicated in the choice. An opal originally placed in the centre had the reputation of shining at night. Because it was unlike any other the opal was known as 'orphanos', and said to be the 'guardian of honour'. Orphanos and a ruby which was once set behind it formed a couple known as 'the stones that guide'. The preponderance of sapphires among the myriad emeralds, amethysts, rubies and pearls reminds us that as symbols of strength they afforded protection against many diseases, including cardiac weaknesses. The figures enamelled on gold plaques represent the emperor's fabulous predecessors, the prophet-kings David and Solomon, hinting at the mixture of religious power with the temporal; furthermore the imperial crown was worn with a mitre whose design derived from those of the bishops.

Later the instruments of coronation multiplied. The sceptre – the judge's staff – symbolized the ruler's judiciary power and took its origin in Ancient Egypt. The treasure of Tutankhamen, among others, includes the two sceptres the pharaoh held: the whip to stimulate his subjects, and the hook to restrain them, in good time, with wise words. The orb, descended from the cosmic sphere of Antiquity, an image of inhabited and uninhabited lands as well as of all Creation, symbolizes the emperor's domination of the world – here a Christian world subjected to the cross which surmounts the orb.

The sword symbolizes the ruler's military authority. It testifies to the fact that the most venerable dynasties earned their thrones by feats of arms. It reminds us that the law of the strongest always prevails. The harshness of this reminder is mitigated by the legend that it was an angel from Heaven who handed Charlemagne the sword that later was used in the coronation of all the Holy Roman emperors. Was it in fact a gift from the Caliph of Baghdad, Harun-Al-Rashid? Or had it belonged to the King of the Huns, Attila himself? Here the truth is even more romantic than the legend.

Crown, sceptre, orb and sword, the indispensable instruments of coronation, form the nucleus of the jewels of every king or queen. Others were later added, including bracelets, symbols of sincerity and wisdom, such as those used by Elizabeth II at her coronation, spurs, an emblem of chivalry, and the ring, cousin to the pastoral ring, symbol of the ruler's mystical union.

The mantle worn at his coronation by the Holy Roman Emperor, the champion of Christianity, paradoxically bears inscriptions in Arabic, the language of the infidels, Christendom's worst enemies. They are the result of a whim on the part of Frederick II, a nonconformist emperor of the twelfth century who bore Muslim civilization a justified admiration.

Finally there is the ampulla, a precious vessel containing the Holy Chrism used to anoint the sovereign in order to confer upon him a sacred character and to make him unique and inviolable. Of all the ampullas none was so sacred as the one used in the coronation of the kings of France, for it had been given by the Holy Spirit to St Remi in order that he anoint Clovis, the first Christian king of France, in 496. The Revolution could not leave such relics of the cursed past in existence. On the afternoon of 7 October 1793, in the presence of the inhabitants of Reims, the city where the kings of France were crowned, Commissaire Ruhl smashed the sacred ampulla on the pedestal of the statue of Louis XV.

After the restoration of the monarchy the fragments of the ampulla, containing the miraculously preserved remains of the Holy Chrism, reappeared – no less miraculously – in order to serve in the coronation of the last king of France, Charles X, in 1825. Blind faith was needed to believe that the sacred ampulla, one of the most venerable and ancient relics of Christendom, had not been completely destroyed. And yet, only a few years ago, rumours began to circulate to the effect that Commissaire Ruhl had shattered a fake ampulla, and that the real one had been preserved and was to this day hidden away

4 Imperial Cross. This cross in gilded silver, precious stones, pearls and engraved plaques, was commissioned in the eleventh century by the Holy Roman Emperor, Henry II. It originally contained the two most precious relics of the Empire: a piece of the True Cross and the point of the Holy Lance. Whether it was the lance used to pierce Christ's side on the Cross, Saint Maurice's lance or the lance which Emperor Constantine held when he had the revelation which made him convert to Christianity, is not known. Certainly, the relic has always been surrounded by an extraordinary aura, and possession of it has been linked to the spiritual power of the Holy Roman Emperor.

5 Crown of Empress Kunigunde. Empress Kunigunde of Luxembourg and her husband, the Holy Roman Emperor Henry II of the House of Bavaria, who ruled in the eleventh century, were both renowned for their piety and both were canonized after their deaths. She wore this crown, one of the oldest remaining in Europe; made of gold, it is attractively decorated with squares and rounds and set with large sapphires and small rubies, amethysts and pearls. As a sign of devotion, she offered the crown to a monastery.

somewhere in safety. According to the same rumours certain historians may have traced the path of the mystery all the way to General de Gaulle – and lost it.

No instrument of coronation in Europe had a prestige or an aura approaching that of the Crown of Charlemagne. Its mere possession constituted a sort of legitimacy, a conferral of power. No one could call himself emperor who did not have the crown. There was in theory only one emperor, and all the kings in the world were no more than his vassals. The latter were determined to contest this state of affairs. 'National' dynasties emerging from the swamps of feudal seigniories pushed back their neighbours' boundaries, nibbling province after province, and carved out their own kingdoms. Profiting by the weakness of the Empire of the West and making use of its internal wars and quarrels of succession, these new masters cut themselves off from their theoretical suzerain, the emperor. They adopted or garnered the title of king and had themselves crowned, and for this purpose made crowns and other instruments of coronation for which they claimed fabulously ancient origins which lent some legitimacy to their power. Little by little the crowns became the pallia of these emergent dynasties, the emblems of embryonic nationalisms or at least of a sense of independent identity.

England saw the implantation of a foreign dynasty from Anjou, the Plantagenets (1154–1485). When it became expedient the monks of Westminster conferred upon them the conveniently rediscovered crown of Edward the Confessor, their prestigious predecessor. This jewel, in fact of later origin, and curiously topped by two bells, was first used in the coronation of Edward II. He conceived the not altogether happy notion of having his current favourite wear it during the ceremony, thereby sparking grumblings that were to grow over the years with each of his successive favourites and eventually to cause his downfall and murder. The first 'Crown of St Edward' was to be used in the coronation of all the kings of England until Charles I.

In Scotland in the sixteenth century the weak James V claimed that the lovely crown he had ordered had been fashioned with the fragments of that of Robert Bruce, his formidable predecessor.

The Capetians, lowly lords who were elected kings, founded a hereditary dynasty (987–1328) and created the nucleus of France. In order to forge a link back to the great and long-extinct Carolingian dynasty, in the early twelfth century King Philip II Augustus produced a crown which he claimed had been the crown of Charlemagne. A heavy jewel set with rubies, emeralds and sapphires, and decorated with fleurs-de-lys, it served in the coronation of twenty-three kings of France.

'It scratches', said Henry III, who was to die at the hands of an assassin. 'It's uncomfortable', said Louis XVI, who was to die at the guillotine.

In the fourteenth century the King of Bohemia, Charles of Luxembourg, crowned the gold bust of St Wenceslas, the pious evangelist and father of Bohemia. Made even more venerable by a relic of the Crown of Thorns set inside it, the jewel, known thenceforth as the 'Crown of St Wenceslas', became linked to the country's independence – though less so than the crown of neighbouring Hungary. The latter was supposed to have served in the coronation of St Stephen the evangelist, the 'founder' of Hungary; in fact it might have been given by a Byzantine emperor to a successor of St Stephen. Over the centuries it came to be considered the pallium of the nation. It had its own guards and was taken out only surrounded by extraordinary pomp. No one could call himself master of Hungary without having been crowned with it. Until the loss of her independence in 1794, Poland crowned her kings with the jewel used in the tenth century by her first king, Boleslaus I. No one would have dared to admit that the real crown of Boleslaus I had disappeared shortly after his death or that the one that bore his name had been fashioned for one of his successors four centuries later.

In 1547, at the age of seventeen, Ivan IV the Terrible proclaimed himself first Tsar of Russia and crowned himself. Without hesitation he dated his crown from the tenth century and chose for its creator his distant predecessor Vladimir Monomakh, the grandson of a Byzantine emperor. Thanks to this the Russian Empire could claim to be heir to Byzantium, enabling Moscow to become the third Rome after Constantinople.

Thus, while 'nations' sprouted like mushrooms over medieval Europe, there appeared in order to legitimize their kings instruments of coronation that were laden with a prestigious past, imbued with holiness and pious legends. These came to form the nuclei of the Crown Jewels of the European dynasties.

Emblems of monarchy, these jewels were in turn destroyed by the anti-monarchistic revolutions. Oliver Cromwell's regime had the so-called Crown of St Edward and other English jewels melted down; the French Revolution was to do the same with the second so-called Crown of Charlemagne. The more pragmatic Bolsheviks at first thought of selling all the Crown Jewels of Russia – Trotsky had them inventoried for this purpose – but, out of some curious respect for the past they had abolished, they kept certain pieces, not the most financially valuable ones, but those most deeply imbued with history.

Emblems of nations, the Crown Jewels were treated as such. Having grabbed the lion's share during the partition of Poland in 1794, the King of Prussia quickly moved the Crown Jewels of Poland, symbols of that nation's former independence, into his care; years later, brought to the verge of ruin by the Napoleonic wars, he did not hesitate to melt them down in order to rescue his finances. However, he had not taken everything,

6 The Peregrina Pearl. This pearl is probably the most famous in the world. Legend has it that it was the sister of the pearl that Queen Cleopatra dissolved in vinegar to use as an aphrodisiac for her lover, Antony. In fact, it was found in the Gulf of Panama by a black slave who won his freedom as a result. Philip II of Spain acquired it, and offered it to his wife, Mary Tudor Queen of England; at her death the pearl came back to Spain. From then on it was worn by successive kings and queens of Spain. At the time of Napoleon's occupation of Spain in 1808, the Peregrina disappeared. Years after Napoleon's fall, not one Peregrina reappeared but three. One of them still belongs to the Spanish royal family. Another was the pride of the collection of the famous Prince Youssoupoff, Rasputin's assassin. The third, illustrated here and perhaps the most authentic, belonged to the Duke of Abercorn.

and among the items left behind was the legendary sword of the kings of Poland, which bore the name 'Szczerbiec'. At the time of the German invasion in 1939 the sword and the other remaining royal treasures were moved to Cracow, then to Rumania, then to France, and finally to Canada, where they were put under lock and key in two convents in Quebec. After the Second World War the communist government of Poland asked, without success, for their restitution. It took fifteen years of laborious negotiations before what remained of the Crown Jewels of Poland was returned to the Royal Palace in Cracow. The West had been far more amenable to sacrificing to the communists the legitimate Polish Government in exile than it was to relinquishing a few objects symbolic of Poland's independence.

Today communist Czechoslovakia exhibits as a relic the crown of the former kings of Bohemia, the Crown of St Wenceslas, in the Cathedral of St Vitus in Prague, the most venerable sanctuary in the country. Late in 1944, when the Soviet armies laid siege to Budapest, the Crown of St Stephen was removed from the strongroom of the Royal Palace and taken out of Hungary in a mysterious special train. Sheltered in a castle near Salzburg, it fell into the hands of the American army. It was taken to the United States and locked up in Fort Knox, where it was kept as a sort of hostage against the communist government of Hungary. After years of negotiations, on 4 January 1978 the American Secretary of State himself travelled to Budapest to deliver to the communist authorities the crown of the former kings of Hungary.

The end of the Middle Ages was also the end of the theoretical pre-eminence of the Holy Roman Emperor over the kings. At the very moment when Charles V managed to restore to the lacklustre empire some of its lost prestige and extended his dominion so far and wide that it never saw the sun set, his rival the King of France, Francis I, declared himself emperor in his own realm and had his crown 'closed'. Until then only the emperor

7 Decoration of the Golden Fleece. In the eighteenth century the ancient orders of chivalry were nothing more than sumptuous jewels that princes swapped from kingdom to kingdom and with which they liked to cover themselves. As witness is this decoration from the Spanish branch of the medieval order of the Golden Fleece. Encrusted with diamonds and a large sapphire, it belonged to the son-in-law of the king of Spain, John VI of Portugal.

Opposite
8 The Goslar Reliquary. This extraordinary object is composed of a cup in agate dating from the Roman epoch which was set in gold in the tenth or eleventh century and then used as a reliquary for the skull of a saint. It was encrusted with two diadems of gold and precious stones, one a simple band, the other a sumptuous closed crown. It is thought that these two crowns belonged to the Imperial German dynasty of Hohenstaufen, and that they came originally from the pillage of a German cathedral.

had been allowed a crown topped with arches, symbols of his worldwide domination; kings had to be content with open crowns. Imitating Francis I, the kings of Europe hurried to close their own crowns, at least on their coats-of-arms. Then they set about quarrelling over precedence, using threats, assassinations of ambassadors, and even the beginnings of wars. They agreed at least to leave the lowest rank to their Polish colleague, not a hereditary but an elected king, and for this reason to forbid him to top his crown with the orb and the cross. Symbolism at least retained its rights.

The Renaissance also saw the disappearance of medieval mysticism. It was replaced by a more pragmatic spirit, specifically the spirit of lucre. Entire families of bankers emerged to build gigantic fortunes, and pushed the spirit of collection to heretofore unequalled heights. What were their clients, the kings, to do? They became collectors as well. And now what were the bankers to do? They became kings, or near-kings. The Fugger family, the bankers of Charles V, were made Princes of the Holy Empire. The Medici obtained the title of Grand-Duke of Tuscany, which made them ruling princes. In the meantime the seeds of the collector's spirit planted by the bankers flourished in the kings. Until then the Crown Jewels had consisted primarily of the instruments of

coronation, reliquaries and other sacred objects. From the Renaissance onward they received the addition of collections of various objects of a purely precious nature.

First came the precious stones – sapphires, emeralds, rubies. Diamonds too had their vogue, especially after the seventeenth century, when Cardinal Mazarin, a fierce and relentless collector, introduced the modern fashion of cutting them to make them sparkle as much as possible. The most beautiful and therefore most coveted of the gems went through many a fantastic adventure, and were often given names. Among the diamonds that have survived to this day are the Regent, the Sancy, the Dresden Green, the Wittelsbach Blue, the Orloff, the Mazarins, the Harlequin, the Grande Condé, the Portuguese and the Swan. Other famous stones are the Black Prince's Ruby, the 'Rubis Côte de Bretagne', the 'Pearl of the Palatinate', half black and half white, a unique fluke, and the Peregrina, the famous pearl of the kings of Spain.

Secondly came the jewels: men's and women's necklaces, pendants, bracelets, earrings, brooches, diadems. The pearls of the necklace given by Pope Clement VII to his niece Catherine de Medici on her marriage to the Dauphin of France were said to be the most beautiful in the world. Passed on to Catherine's daughter-in-law, Mary Queen of Scots, the jewel was later bought by her rival Elizabeth I, and remains in the possession of her successor Elizabeth II. Kings soon made jewels of the ancient orders of knighthood: badges of the Holy Spirit glittering with diamonds; pendants of the Golden Fleece swollen with enormous gems; Garters or Elephants of Denmark in enamelled gold; decorations of Bavaria, Saxony or Russia set with emeralds or rubies.

Last came the objects. Jewellers, most of them Italian or German, worked their gold with dazzling skill into the strangest of shapes and covered them with sparkling enamels. They took ostrich eggs, coconuts, coral branches, rhinoceros horn, rare seashells or baroque pearls, and transformed them into fantastic animals or grotesque human figures. They carved ivory, rock crystal, amethyst, topaz, jade, carnelian, agates, heliotrope, chalcedony, jasper, lapis lazuli and amber, into cups, statuettes, vases, urns and platters. They set antique cameos into jewelboxes or mounted them as jewels. Most of these masterpieces served no purpose other than to delight the eye. But the goldsmiths also used precious materials to make useful objects – chandeliers, inkwells, mirrors, boxes, scissors, thimbles and so on. The fashion of the precious object soon extended to furniture: tables of marble and semi-precious stones, amber cabinets, solid silver furniture, vermeil consoles or flower-pot holders. The King of Denmark ordered himself a throne of unicorn-horn (it was in fact made from tusks of the narwhal) and three life-size lions of silver. The Russian Tsar held audiences from a throne of gold set with rubies and turquoise.

Jewels that were objects by virtue of their size and function, or objects that were jewels in the richness of their materials, these various 'curiosities' assembled by the kings were joined to the precious stones and the actual jewels to form a body – the Crown Jewels, the Treasures of the Crown. Carefully inventoried, they were given a status – property of the State or property of the Crown (then intrinsically linked). Handed down from ruler to ruler, from generation to generation to the head of the family, they were indivisible and incommunicable. They were the highest gratification of the royal collector, but they also contributed to the ruler's prestige; and, although it generally remained unsaid, they were also something in hand in times of crisis or penury. In

9 The Phoenix Jewel of Elizabeth I.
Probably no woman in history has worn
as many jewels as Elizabeth I of England.
Perhaps she wanted to hide, beneath her
layers of jewels, a personal insecurity
which combined strangely with her
political genius. In each of her portraits,
she is dripping in jewels, almost none of
which survived Oliver Cromwell's
regime. The only witnesses to her
splendour are the numerous richly set
cameos and medallions which bear her
famous profile. Among them is this
jewel, made in gold surrounded by red
and white Tudor roses in enamel, and
bearing on its back the emblem she
chose, the phoenix, the bird that can be
reborn from its ashes.

principle they were not at anyone's disposal, least of all that of their owner the king; but the king often did sell or pawn them. The Queen of Castille, Isabella the Catholic, is supposed to have pawned her necklace of balas rubies in order to fund Christopher Columbus's expedition. King Christian IV of Denmark pawned in Hamburg the marvellous crown he had ordered with infinite care. Queen Henrietta Maria, exiled and ruined wife of Charles I, sold in Paris several diamonds of the Crown of England. Thus, these supposedly incommunicable jewels became great travellers; crowns were handed from moneylender to moneylender, precious stones from collector to collector.

Among the collectors, the Tudors distinguished themselves by a hunger for precious objects worthy of the Medici, a dynasty in everything but name. Jewel-mad Henry VIII seized the treasures of the monasteries which he dissolved in the 1530s, and ordered from Hans Holbein, his Court painter, 179 designs of jewels. His daughter Elizabeth I probably remains the woman who wore the most jewels at a time; all her portraits show her covered in them. She bought up those of her imprisoned rival Mary Queen of Scots, kept the jewels of the Crown of Portugal, pawned by an unlucky pretender, as well as those of the Crown of Navarre 'mortgaged' by Henry VI. For the Habsburgs, an august dynasty, artistry and rarity took precedence over glitter. In his city of Prague, the Mecca of magic, Rudolph II, an aficionado of astrology reeking of heresy, accumulated extraordinary pieces of jewellery and supposedly magical knick-knacks. His cousin Archduke Ferdinand of Tirol indulged more deeply in the bizarre, collecting in his castle at Ambras both natural grotesques and set-pieces of great refinement. Both collections now languish in neglected rooms of the Kunsthistorisches Museum in Vienna.

Three generations of Danish kings in the sixteenth and seventeenth centuries, Christian IV, Frederick III and Christian V, bought piece after piece and assembled one of the most complete and most beautiful sets of Renaissance jewellery and ornaments, to which were added many excellent jewels in the eighteenth century. This treasure is admirably exhibited amidst the enchanting and unbelievable muddle in the Castle of Rosenborg near Copenhagen. In Sweden in the mid-sixteenth century the tragic king,

Eric XIV, ordered instruments of coronation of admirable beauty and richness, the nucleus of the present Crown Jewels of Sweden. Suspected of insanity, he was deposed, imprisoned and condemned to death; he died in prison shortly before he was to be executed, probably poisoned by his brother.

The wise Wittelsbachs, in the person of Duke Albert V of Bavaria, assembled in the sixteenth century the nucleus of a collection of jewellery matchless in richness. Enhanced by a unique series of precious objects of the Middle Ages, and further endowed in the nineteenth century by sumptuous ornaments, it is to this day probably the most important treasure in Europe. It is displayed in Munich at the Residence, which was faithfully reconstructed after the Second World War. In the eighteenth century, a German ruler formidable in all respects – it is said he sired three hundred bastards – Augustus the Strong, Elector of Saxony, gave enormous orders to a goldsmith of wizardry, Dinglinger. With the richest materials Dinglinger constructed objects of utmost extravagance, unequalled examples of the most reckless – and well-paid – baroque. Priceless knick-knacks, famous diamonds, ornaments of every known type of stone accumulated in the famous Green Vault of the Royal Palace in Dresden. After their removal by the Soviet army in 1945, they were more or less all returned and eventually once again exhibited in the Saxon capital.

In Russia the Tsaritsas of the eighteenth century, Elizabeth and then Catherine II, began a collection of jewels that was to be enlarged by all their successors down to the last Tsar Nicholas II. The quality, variety and quantity of the stones soon provided the Russian Court with a reputation for surpassing any other at any time. Exhibited in enormous vitrines in the Tsaritsas' bedrooms, or worn by the numerous grand duchesses who changed two or three times every evening, these jewels dazzled even the most surfeited visitors, including the maharajas who were reputed to be the greatest collectors of jewels in the world.

The most dedicated collector in seventeenth-century Europe was Louis XIV. He enlarged the collection begun by Francis I, and made of it the then-uncontested first collection of the world. He bought 9,795 pearls from the Queen of Poland, 45 large diamonds and 1,122 small ones from Tavernier, 14 large and 131 small from another merchant – and so on and so forth until the end of his long reign. Snatching up everything he could find, Louis XIV displayed the collector's most indispensable quality, greed. He bought up for a low price the diamonds of his own aunt Queen Henrietta Maria of England, then in exile, whom he maintained in miserable poverty. When, feeling the approach of death, he decided to stage a farewell show for his court and the world, he used the pretext of an audience with a Persian ambassador to have an enormous amount of diamonds and pearls sewn on his clothes; they were so heavy that he staggered under their weight.

The dawning eighteenth century saw a revolution in feminine fashions. Until then even the most extravagant women had limited themselves to a small number of heavy, sumptuously trimmed dresses which they wore time and time again. Suddenly it struck them as necessary to wear light dresses and change them as often as possible. This fashion had an effect on jewels, including those of the crown. Respect demanded that the sacred crowns of the Middle Ages be kept; but since they seemed so terribly old-fashioned, the kings took to designing lighter and more elegant ones for each coronation. Having returned to the throne of England in 1660, the Stuarts reconstituted a (false) Crown of St Edward in order to re-establish their link with tradition; but each new ruler, down to the present Queen, ordered a new crown to don immediately after the coronation with the Crown of St Edward. Each king of France, after receiving the (second) venerable Crown of Charlemagne, exchanged it for a new crown fashioned for the coronation, glittering with his very best stones.

Everywhere in Europe the diamonds of the crowns, removed after use, were re-set according to the latest dictates of fashion. Queen Marie Antoinette sometimes had the Regent, her most beautiful stone, taken out and gracefully pinned it in her hair. Then came the French Revolution. Marie Antoinette was locked up in the prison of the Temple in Paris with the royal family to await judgment and execution. The Regent, with the other Crown Jewels, was put in the Garde-Meubles National, located in one of the two pavilions on the Place de la Concorde, and official seals were put on the doors. During the night of 15 September 1792, when Paris was in the throes of the terrible September massacres, a patrol hurried across the Place de la Concorde. The officer leading the patrol suddenly noticed the strange shadow cast by one of the four street-lamps around. Raising his eyes, he saw a man straddling the iron bracket. Threatened with the soldiers' rifles, the acrobat slithered down and without hesitation told his story. He was part of a band of robbers who had climbed the lamp-post, vaulted on to the balcony of the Garde-Meubles, broken through a window and made off with the Crown Jewels. Horror-struck, the servants of the young Republic entered the Garde-Meubles and found a desert: none of the 8,000 diamonds of the Crown was left. The burglars had taken their time, returning several nights in a row, and even pausing for picnics of sausage and wine. They were so laden with booty that they had sprinkled precious stones all over the Place de la Concorde. After a desperate search about 1,500 diamonds were recovered, among them such famous ones as the Regent and the Sancy. The others – including several stones known the world over – are still at large.

It was in a sense the fate of the treasures of the kings to excite people's greed and to be dispersed or disappear. In 1671 a daring burglar, Captain Blood, stole the Crown of England from the Tower of London. Rather than let him be executed after his arrest, Charles II, amazed by his boldness, offered him a post in his guard. Even our era, with its ultra-sophisticated security systems, is not safe from such hazards. A few years ago four robbers entered the Galerie d'Apollon at the Louvre in the rush-hour and stole from its case the coronation sword of Charles X, the last King of France. The sword, inlaid with 1,576 diamonds, has never been found.

What was not stolen was sometimes dispersed in enormous sales, conducted more for political than financial reasons. In 1887 the Third Republic sold most of the Crown Jewels of France, which had been reassembled after the Revolution of 1789. Similarly, the Soviets sold an enormous amount of the Crown Jewels of Russia in 1927. This practice, though far removed from the vandalism of the regime of Cromwell or the French Revolution, destroyed many an admirable ensemble.

Other treasures were pawned and never recovered by their owners. The Crown Jewels of Savoy, 'mortgaged' in Amsterdam, were simply annexed in 1795 by the French army of invasion and were never returned to the dukes of Savoy. During the struggle for the unification of Italy, Francis II, the last King of the Two Sicilies, pawned the Crown

10 **Silver Baptismal Font.** In the seventeenth century, at the time of the Reformation, objects which were linked to the royal 'liturgy' became excessively sumptuous. This baptismal font of solid silver, chiselled by a French silversmith in 1695, was commissioned by Charles XI of Sweden, the founder of the absolute Swedish monarchy. This energetic sovereign had a brilliant and prosperous reign and was the father of the famous Charles XII, who was baptized in this font. Since then it has served at the baptism of all the members of the Swedish royal family, including the children of the present monarchs, King Carl Gustaf and Queen Sylvia.

Jewels in order to levy more troops. Vanquished despite the heroic resistance of his wife Queen Maria, exiled and ruined, he was not able to raise enough money to redeem his jewels, which languish to this day in the vault of a Baron Rothschild descended from the moneylender.

Yet other treasures vanished without a trace. Deposed by a socialist revolution in 1918, the last Emperor of Austria fled into exile with an important part of the Crown Jewels, which were considered his personal property. Among these objects were the Empress's crown of diamonds and pearls, several invaluable sets of jewellery and four diamonds of historical importance. Strange rumours have circulated ever since, according to which some of the jewels were discreetly sold in order to finance attempts at restoring the Emperor, while others were entrusted to a confidence man who simply left for South America with the treasure and disappeared. The fact is that no one has heard of those jewels since, even though they were important, numerous, inventoried and even photographed.

Nothing is more mysterious than the fate of the Crown Jewels of Spain. At the beginning of the nineteenth century, Charles IV, sensing the arrival of the Napoleonic storm, had his beloved collection of clocks walled up in one of the rooms of the Royal Palace. His splendid collection of jewels was hidden in the wall of another room. A servant carefully kept samples of the draperies of both rooms in order to remember which they were. As predicted, Napoleon invaded Spain, occupied it and placed his brother Joseph on the throne. In 1814 the legitimate king, the horrible Ferdinand VII, son of Charles IV, recovered his throne – and the two samples which the faithful servant handed him. Alas! During his short reign the usurper Joseph Bonaparte had changed all the draperies in the Royal Palace and no one remembered in which rooms the precious collections had been immured. Faced with the choice of having all the walls of his 360-room palace ripped open or writing off his treasure, Ferdinand VII opted for the second solution. Over the years the story of the walled-up treasure became a legend in which no one really believed any more, until a few decades ago some plumbers working in the Royal Palace brought Charles IV's collection of clocks to light. So the story had to be true. If the clocks were there, then the jewels too must be hidden somewhere. But how to find them? To this day no one has come up with an answer.

The French Revolution had dealt a death-blow to the European monarchies, to their sacred character, to their very meaning. The concept of the Crown Jewels was to bear the consequences of the change. Surrounded by mystique in the Middle Ages, mere collections after the Renaissance, altered by the fashions of the eighteenth century, they fell into vanity in the nineteenth. Napoleon, the successor to as well as the victor of the Revolution, made himself emperor. He was obviously thinking of Charlemagne: he summoned the Pope to crown him and he ordered the manufacture of a crown – a simple affair of gilded silver set with modest cameos – which he dubbed, without the slightest justification, the 'Crown of Charlemagne'. In the event neither Pope nor crown were used: Napoleon crowned himself with a gold crown of laurels. To top it all off he made an oath to hold undivided all the territory 'of the Republic', thus maintaining the ambiguous status of the brand-new 'empire'.

The superb ceremony was not spared its farcical incidents. Repentant former revolutionaries and military men risen from the ranks became tangled in the protocol to which their past had not accustomed them. Napoleon's sisters, furious at having to carry the new empress Josephine's train, dropped it suddenly, almost causing Josephine to topple backwards. Napoleon's mother had quarrelled with him and refused to appear, but Napoleon forced the painter J. L. David to place her in full view in the painting of the ceremony. In short the whole operation was quite different from the esoteric, symbolism-laden coronations of the past.

Napoleon repeated the ceremony in Milan to have himself crowned King of Italy, for which he ordered a new set of Crown Jewels. Thereupon he started making kings right and left. He made kings of his brothers and brothers-in-law, and promoted the representatives of the oldest dynasties of Germany, counting on the legendary vanity of the German princes. Bavaria, Saxony and Württemberg became kingdoms. Prussia had become one a century before; the Holy Roman Emperor Leopold I, needing the armies of the Elector of Brandenburg to fight Louis XIV, and having nothing tangible to offer in exchange, had hit on the idea of making him king in 1700. Wild with happiness, Frederick I had ordered a superb crown, run to Königsberg to be crowned King of Prussia, and become the Emperor's faithful ally.

The rulers elevated by Napoleon, the kings of Bavaria and Saxony and the grand-dukes of Baden and Mecklenburg, placed orders with the best jewellers of their time for lovely instruments of coronation which they set with the best stones of their treasure. The richness of these jewels could not erase the slightly inglorious promotion of their owners who, besides, did not dare to have themselves crowned. During the ceremony of their accession they limited themselves to placing the instruments of coronation on a stool next to their throne. Thus they inaugurated the tradition of the Crown Jewels as trinkets, and were followed in this path by a number of kingdoms which appeared in the nineteenth century and even more recently. The current Queen Beatrix of Holland and the current kings of Spain and Sweden were enthroned with their crowns placed on a cushion beside them. Certain democratic kingdoms such as Denmark and Greece did not even display their crowns at the accession of the new ruler, but only on their predecessor's coffin. 'New' kingdoms such as Belgium and Italy did not even bother to order crowns.

In the Balkans in the nineteenth century dynasties imported from abroad or issued from *coups d'état* made touching attempts to forge links back to the glorious past. In Serbia the Karajeorgevich family had a crown fashioned with the metal of a cannon that had been seized from the Turks, their traditional enemy. In Rumania the Hohenzollerns did the same for the king's crown, while beautiful Queen Maria had a medieval Byzantine crown copied for hers. In Bulgaria Tsar Ferdinand simply had his portrait painted with the crown he dreamed of donning in Constantinople. The picturesque had arrived, and the exotic was not long in coming.

Maximilian of Austria, Emperor of Mexico, Pedro I of Braganza, Emperor of Brazil, and Henri Christophe, the Black Emperor of Haiti, all ordered very elaborate crowns, which are still kept in their respective countries, testimony mostly to the fleeting quality of their empires. The Queen of Hawaii and the Queen of Madagascar both had their crowns. One thing led to another, and eventually came to a climax with the farce of 'Emperor' Bokassa of Central Africa who, in spite of the highly tangible value of the jewels of his crown, ridiculed monarchies, coronations and crowns.

The twentieth century has seen the fall of quite a number of European monarchies.

Left **11 Victoria Eugenia,** grand-daughter of Queen Victoria, god-daughter of Empress Eugénie, was named after both. She married Alfonso XIII of Spain. This photograph shows her on the terrace of the Royal Palace in Madrid, in Court dress, wearing a small diamond crown.

Right **12 Elizabeth II** at her coronation in Westminster Abbey in 1953. The photograph was taken just after the Archbishop of Canterbury had placed St Edward's Crown on her head.

Only a few remain, stripped of their power but imbued with a prestige they often lacked in former times. The instruments of coronation are hardly ever used. Crowns and sceptres are simply trinkets honoured at funerals and accessions. Only Britain still makes full use of them at coronations and the Opening of Parliament.

Like the monarchies, the Crown Jewels have come to the end of their adventures. Once the object of rivalry and quarrels, once the source of many a tragedy, those that have not been destroyed, stolen or sold now rest quietly in museums. Yet their prestige, evident in their attraction for tourism, has never been greater. In the palaces of European capitals no exhibits draw more spectators than those of the treasure-rooms. After standing patiently in line for hours the crowds jostle one another to glimpse, albeit for a few seconds, the glittering objects, in order to dream at length, later, of the Crown Jewels.

We shall now start our tour through Europe from treasure to treasure. As you will see, we have cut out of our itinerary certain past and present kingdoms. Recent and highly democratic monarchies such as Belgium and Luxembourg never ordered any Crown Jewels. The principality of Monaco has never had any. The Balkan kingdoms had crowns but today they are practically inaccessible and their mediocre artistic interest does not encourage us to force the doors of the safes where they are kept.

The Holy Roman Empire and Austria

*I*n the year 800 Pope Leo III literally invented the Empire of the West for Charlemagne, by his act of crowning him in St Peter's, Rome. But Charlemagne's
Carolingian dynasty was soon to fail. His son and successor Louis the Pious divided the
Empire between his three rebellious sons. One was given France, another Germany; the
eldest, Lothair, received Lotharingia, an area named after him. Lotharingia was the
ancestor of Lorraine, a buffer-state that was to be the cause of endless quarrels and wars
between France and Germany.

In the tenth century Otto I the Great founded a smaller but more coherent version of
the empire, the Holy Roman Empire. The principal dynasties that were to inherit it –
Saxons, Franconians, Hohenstaufen and Luxembourg – produced a few great sovereigns
who singlehandedly maintained the strength and unity of the empire. Each emperor had
to stand up to all his unlucky competitors, for he was elected. He had to fight the pope, the
other 'Half of God', who disputed his power; the German princes, who were placed
under his direct authority and did their utmost to wear it down; and the kings of Europe,
theoretically his vassals, who thought only of contesting his suzerainty. Thus anarchy
reappeared every time a weak ruler sat on the throne.

The Habsburgs came to the Imperial throne in the fifteenth century. Originally minor
lords of a Swiss canton, they had acquired in the eleventh century the County of
Habsburg. It was two centuries before Rudolph of Habsburg, elected King of Germany,
invested his sons with the Duchy of Austria. The family was to make the great leap when
Frederick III of Habsburg was elected Roman Emperor. Now that they held the Empire,
the Habsburgs were never to let go. While maintaining the fiction of Imperial election
they transformed it into an increasingly meaningless formality which in fact disguised a
hereditary succession. They also instituted a policy of fabulous marriages which they
pursued with ability akin to genius. Through these marriages they inherited the immense
fortune of the dukes of Burgundy as well as the kingdoms of Bohemia and Hungary. The
Habsburgs died out with their last emperor, Charles VI, in 1740; his heiress, however, his

13 Imperial Orb. This orb of gold, diamonds and precious stones dates from the twelfth century. A symbol
of worldwide domination, it served in the coronation of the Holy Roman Emperors. When in 1806
Napoleon abolished the Holy Roman Empire, its last head, henceforth Francis I Emperor of Austria, took
the orb and the other instruments of coronation to Vienna, where they have remained as museum pieces.

daughter Empress Maria Theresa, who married the Duke of Lorraine, kept the name for herself and her descendants.

When Napoleon proclaimed himself Emperor of the French in 1804, Francis I of Habsburg sensed that his Holy Roman Empire was not long for this world. Anticipating the plans of the 'Corsican ogre', he named himself 'Hereditary Emperor of Austria', which struck his contemporaries as incongruous. At any rate his predictions proved accurate, for in 1806 Napoleon dissolved the thousand-year-old, weary Holy Empire.

The Austrian Empire was to last more than a century. The Allies dismantled it in 1918, and a socialist revolution ran the Habsburgs out of Austria, beginning an era of instability in Central Europe which has not yet come to an end. Now that they have left the stage, history has been compelled to recognize that the Habsburgs and their empire·were once a remarkable stabilizing and moderating influence.

Three rulers in particular are responsible for the treasure of the Habsburgs: chivalrous Maximilian I, strange Rudolph II and Empress Maria Theresa, a bold and wise mother-hen.

The jumble of the precious collections housed in Vienna, at the Hofburg and the Kunsthistorisches Museum, testifies to the tossed destiny of the Habsburgs. There is a part of the Crown Jewels of the Holy Roman Empire, kept after its abolition, by the last emperor Francis I. There are the beautiful remains of the treasure of the dukes of Burgundy. Finally there are the Crown Jewels of the Austrian Empire: the Habsburgs considered them their private property, but nevertheless left the finest pieces behind when they fled Austria.

14 Crown of Charlemagne

This crown of gold, enamel, pearls and precious stones, the most venerable of all the crowns in the world, was never used by Charlemagne. It was made for Otto I, the founder of the Holy Roman Empire of Germany, and remodelled by Otto III, who added the gem-studded arch. An emblem of temporal power, it is designed to be worn with a mitre, symbol of spiritual authority.

When in 1938 Hitler annexed Austria he demanded that the crown be brought to Nuremberg from Vienna. In an attempt to defend the crown the Austrian curator pointed out that it carried enamelled portraits of two Jews, David and Solomon. Hitler hesitated, but pressed his demand nonetheless. When the Americans liberated Nuremberg the crown had disappeared. Local Nazi leaders, arrested and questioned, insisted that it had been thrown into the deepest lake in Austria. Unconvinced, the American officers arrested the mayor of Nuremberg who, under considerable pressure, revealed the truth: Himmler himself had given orders to hide the crown and spread the legend of its disappearance. Following the mayor's instructions, the Americans climbed down into a bunker deep underground, where they found, sealed inside a wall, a locked copper chest containing the Crown of Charlemagne. It was returned to Austria, where it remains to this day.

REX
SALOMON

15, 16 Imperial Mantle and Shoes

In the eleventh century Norman adventurers, descended from the Vikings, settled in Sicily, where they founded a kingdom and a dynasty. They created a strange civilization where Western culture mingled with Byzantium and Islam. The harems of the kings of Sicily were Arab; so were the artisans who came from the Middle East to weave their marvellous silks. The Norman King, Roger II, ordered from them this crimson silk mantle embroidered with gold, which they inscribed with Arabic characters and the date of Hegira in which it was made. The mantle was handed down to Roger II's son-in-law Emperor Henry VI, and afterwards served in the coronation of the Holy Roman Emperors. Thus the mantle made and signed by the infidels was used by their enemies, the defenders of Christendom.

The protocol and pomp of the Norman kings of Sicily were also Byzantine. As an emblem of their rank the Byzantine emperors wore crimson shoes embroidered with golden eagles; the kings of Sicily obtained permission from the pope to wear them as well. Their heirs the Holy Roman Emperors inherited the shoes and the custom of wearing them at their coronation.

17 Crown of Emperor Rudolph II

This crown of gold, enamel, pearls, rubies and diamonds, topped with an enormous sapphire, is one of the finest examples of the art of Renaissance goldsmiths. It was fashioned at the order of the strange sixteenth-century emperor, Rudolph II. At Prague, that most magical of cities, he held court among artists and sorcerers, including one of the greatest masters of astrology, Tycho Brahe. The Emperor himself was accused of dabbling in alchemy and magic. He was dethroned, and died insane.

The big pearl on the central panel was found by a native diver in the gulf of Panama in the early sixteenth century. Stolen by the Spanish conquerors of Latin America, it became the property of Emperor Charles V. The other pearls were presents from the Persian ruler Shah Abbas to Rudolph II. Later the crown became the emblem of the Austrian Empire; but it was never used, for the emperors of Austria were not crowned.

18 Imperial Sceptre of Austria

Rudolph's brother and successor Matthias continued his tradition of patronage by ordering admirable jewels from the workshops of Prague, including this sceptre in the style of Rudolph's crown. The handle is made of a narwhal's horn. At the time it was claimed to be unicorn horn, a magic substance. Like Rudolph's crown it is topped with a big sapphire, a stone that was considered excellent protection against disease.

19 *Amethyst of Charles II*

In the seventeenth century amethyst was still a precious stone of great rarity. This one, richly topped with a crown of gold and emeralds, was sent by Charles II of Spain to his cousin, Emperor Leopold I. The ties between the courts of Madrid and Vienna were close, because two branches of the same family had reigned there for over a hundred years, since the time of Emperor Charles V. Charles II, the last, tragic Spanish Habsburg, could sire no children, and throughout his life had to endure the sight of all Europe quarrelling over his succession and planning to carve up his empire. No doubt he wanted to leave his innumerable crowns to his cousins the Austrian Habsburgs. In the end, however, he gave in to ceaseless harrying by the champions of France, and left them to the Duke of Anjou, grandson of Louis XIV. After his death in 1700 this much-contested decision sparked the War of the Spanish Succession, which lasted fourteen years.

20 *La Bella*

This 416-carat hyacinth, set in a two-headed eagle of gold and enamel, was bought in the seventeenth century by Emperor Leopold I from a great family of the Hungarian aristocracy.

21 Cameo of Noah

This cameo belonged not to the Habsburgs but to one of their thirteenth-century predecessors on the German Imperial throne, Frederick II of Hohenstaufen. He was a ruler much ahead of his time, and one of the more curious figures of the Middle Ages. His mother was Sicilian, and he eschewed his nordic Empire to live at Palermo. As Frederick I, King of Sicily, he there assembled an extraordinary court of Arab artists and Jewish scientists, with whom he liked to converse. When the Pope forced him to leave on the Fifth Crusade in 1228, Frederick found it more expedient to make friends with the Arabs than to fight them. He met with the Sultan of Egypt, with whom he shared wide cultural interests, and the Sultan handed over Jerusalem in 1229 without his having to draw his sword. The Pope did not consider this arrangement satisfactory, and excommunicated him.

The cameo shows Noah and his family boarding the Ark. It was carved in Sicily for Frederick, with techniques used in antiquity, and testifies to the high level of artistic skill found at his court. Later it belonged to the Medici prince, Lorenzo the Magnificent, a collector as knowledgeable as Frederick II. In the late eighteenth century it was bought in Paris by the Earl of Carlisle.

22 Elizabeth of Bavaria on the day of her wedding to
Emperor Francis Joseph I in 1854.

23 Zita of Bourbon-Parma, wife of Emperor Charles I of
Austria, at her coronation as Queen of Hungary in Budapest,
1916.

When the Austrian Empire was overthrown by a socialist
revolution in 1918, the Emperor Charles I carried most of the
Crown Jewels, considered his private property, into exile.
Among them were the jewels of Elizabeth of Bavaria and the
crown worn by his wife Empress Zita. Nothing has been
heard of the jewels since, except strange rumours, according
to which some were sold to finance attempts at restoring
Charles I to the throne, and others entrusted to the care of a
close friend of the Imperial family. According to the rumours
this person, instead of putting them in a safe place, took them
to South America, where they disappeared for good.

Germany: Bavaria

The Wittelsbach dynasty appeared in the tenth century, in the person of Arnulf, the cousin of a Carolingian emperor. From the very start it was linked to Bavarian soil. In the twelfth century the Wittelsbachs were dukes of Bavaria, and one of them, Ludwig V, was elected Holy Roman Emperor. Kings by the grace of Napoleon after 1805, the Wittelsbachs lost their throne in a republican coup in 1918; but they still reside in Bavaria, where they enjoy a position of privilege, surrounded by the respect and affection of their former subjects. The insanity attributed to them is a recent inheritance from the House of Prussia. In fact the Wittelsbachs were wise and paternal administrators, knowledgeable patrons and fierce collectors, who prospered side by side with their opulent Bavaria.

The treasure (it remains under their partial ownership) is exhibited at the Residenz Palace in Munich. It is testimony to the continuity of the Wittelsbachs as well as to the splendour of their taste. The richest collection of jewels in Europe, it ranges from the High Middle Ages to the twentieth century, a matchless showcase for the talents of German, Italian, French and English goldsmiths and jewellers.

24 **Brooch in the shape of a trophy.** This jewel, in the shape of a military trophy, set with pearls and brilliants, was made in the heroic style of the seventeenth century. Long considered one of the most important treasures of the House of Bavaria, it was made for Duke Maximilian I, who is regarded as the father of the Bavarian people, mostly because he protected his states from the Thirty Years' War.

25 Orb of the Kings of Bavaria

In 1806 the Duchy of Bavaria was promoted to Kingdom by Napoleon. The ruling duke, issued from a lesser branch of the House of Bavaria, a former officer in the French Army, who had once been a penurious younger son, suddenly found himself king under the name Maximilian I. From the most famous goldsmith of the era – Biennais, a Frenchman – he ordered magnificent regalia; they were never used, for there was no coronation. He had them set with beautiful gems from the treasures of his House.

26 Crown of Princess Blanche

The royal dignity of Bavaria is relatively recent, but the House of Wittelsbach, which obtained it, is extremely ancient. Evidence of its longevity is furnished by this crown inlaid with sapphires, emeralds, rubies and pearls. Tradition holds that it was first given by the King of France, Charles VI the Mad, to his daughter Isabella when she married Richard II, King of England, in 1396. Richard was deposed and imprisoned and, in 1400, assassinated. His usurper, Henry IV, seized the crown and later gave it to his own daughter, Blanche of Lancaster, on her wedding to a Palatine count of the Rhine from the House of Bavaria. Their distant descendant, Frederick V Elector of Palatine, pretended to the crown of Bohemia in 1619; his wife Elizabeth Stuart, the famous Winter Queen, wore this crown during the brief period when she had the pleasure of being Queen of Bohemia.

27 Parure of Queen Theresa

This parure of rubies and diamonds, one of the finest in the world, includes rubies from the famous collection assembled by the dukes of Bavaria in the eighteenth century. Given by Ludwig I of Bavaria to his wife Theresa of Saxe-Altenburg, one could say it was a consolation prize, for he was constantly and openly unfaithful to her. Ludwig, an utter original, could not set eyes on a pretty woman without falling in love. What recourse did poor Queen Theresa have against the likes of Lola Montez? Bewitched, Ludwig ruined himself for her, forgetting his rank, his wife and Bavaria. Moreover he lost his crown in the affair, when a revolution overthrew him in 1848. Who followed him into exile? Not beautiful Lola Montez, of course, but good Queen Theresa.

28 The Palatinate Pearl

This pearl, mounted between two diamond snakes, is a unique fluke of nature, part white, part black. Its origins are unknown. It first appeared among the treasures of the branch of the House of Bavaria which ruled the Palatinate, from which it derives its name. Having wandered from castle to castle it arrived in Munich in the late eighteenth century with its owner of the time, the Palatine count, Charles Theodore, when he became Duke of Bavaria at the extinction of the older branch of his family.

29 Hat-brooch of Ludwig II

Young, handsome, intelligent and adored, Ludwig II seemed earmarked for success. But madness loomed over him; he ruined himself in order to build extravagant castles, expenses which thoroughly exasperated his subjects, although the castles remain the principal touristic attraction in Bavaria. He had the merit of recognizing the genius of the composer Richard Wagner when the latter was still relatively unknown. His death remains a mystery; dethroned and imprisoned, he was found dead in a lake next to his alienist doctor, whom he had possibly strangled. Ludwig liked to wear this somewhat garish ornament of diamonds and rubies on his hat. The fleur-de-lys in the centre is indicative of his obsession with the Sun King Louis XIV.

30 Crown of the Queens of Bavaria

This crown, made with pearls of extraordinary quality, was ordered for the wife of the first king Maximilian I, Caroline Frederika of Baden; she was openly an adversary of Napoleon, to whom her husband, to her constant humiliation, was pledged. The crown was reset at the order of Ludwig II, who came to the throne in 1864, for his cousin and fiancée Duchess Sophie of Bavaria. He had given her the Wagnerian name Elsa, often had Wagner's operas staged exclusively for the two of them, and in general behaved so strangely that the betrothal had to be broken off. Poor Sophie, who was never to wear the crown of Bavaria, died many years later in a fire.

31 Ludwig III of Bavaria inherited the throne from his cousin the mad king Otto in 1913 and was dethroned in 1918. In this photograph he is wearing the dress of the Order of St George, and is on his way to the chapter of that order.

Germany: Saxony

*T*he ancient dynasty of Wettin, originally from Swabia, was invested with the Duchy of Saxony in the fifteenth century. It then divided into many branches who ruled over tiny duchies. One of them, the Saxe-Weimars, was furiously intellectual and extended its protection to the greatest writers of the time. Another, the Saxe-Coburgs, was to have an exceptional destiny in the nineteenth century, when it occupied, among others, the thrones of England, Belgium, Portugal and Bulgaria. Two dukes of Saxony were successively elected king of Poland in the eighteenth century. Kings, thanks to Napoleon, after 1806, they were dethroned in 1918.

The Wettins' extraordinary collection of jewels and precious objects was assembled mostly by Augustus II the Strong – a ruler obsessed with the example of Louis XIV – who managed in the early eighteenth century to give Dresden unequalled brilliance. The treasure, one of the richest and most extravagant in Europe, was sheltered in the fortress of Königstein, outside Dresden, during the Second World War and escaped the terrible bombing of the city. When the Soviets occupied Saxony a special detachment of their army 'took delivery' of the entire treasure and carried it to Moscow. In 1958 it was at last returned to East Germany, and it is once again exhibited in the Green Vault, which was badly damaged in the War and entirely restored.

32 The Court of Auranzeb. There is no better illustration of the extravagance of Augustus the Strong, or of the talents of his goldsmith, Dinglinger, than this $4\frac{1}{2}$-foot (1.37-metre) long centrepiece of gold, silver, enamel and precious stones. Comprising 132 lilliputian figures all of precious metals, perfect miniature objects and animals, inlaid with 4,909 diamonds, 164 emeralds, 160 rubies, 16 pearls, 2 cameos and one sapphire, it is meant to represent the court of the Great Mogul. In fact, it is a monument to reckless and precious baroque.

33 Pendant with Coats-of-Arms

This jewel, inlaid with 77 diamonds, 28 rubies and 4 emeralds, was carved in 1610 and recalls the fine taste of the German princes for heraldry. It shows the coat-of-arms of the Duchy of Saxony topped by crossed swords, the symbol of the dignity of Elector of the Holy Empire. On the sides, the smaller coats-of-arms of the duchies of Juliers, Cleve and Berg recall the possessions of the House of Saxony.

34 Sword of Augustus the Strong

Imitating Louis XIV, Augustus the Strong had the best stones in his treasure mounted for his personal use. He ordered suites in diamonds, emeralds, rubies, sapphires, cornelian and tortoiseshell. Each of the suites comprised daggers, swords, buttons, snuffboxes, key chains, brooches, buckles, decorations and canes, all of them glittering with precious stones. The photograph shows one of the swords from the emerald suite.

35 The Green Diamond of Dresden

This 41-carat stone, mounted in a shoulder-knot in the eighteenth century, is unique in its apple-green tint. It is also the largest green diamond in the world. It was bought in 1743 at the famous fair of Leipzig by a son of Augustus the Strong, Frederick Elector of Saxony, who was as dedicated a collector as his father. Like the other Crown Jewels, it escaped the bombing of Dresden in the Second World War, and is now exhibited again in the Green Vault.

36 Emerald Order of the White Eagle

In the eighteenth century, and especially among the German princes, old orders of knighthood became jewels for men, pretexts for wearing larger and larger stones. This tendency is illustrated by this plaque of a Polish Order; it was part of a suite belonging to Augustus the Strong, who had awarded himself the order upon being elected King of Poland in 1697. It did not prevent him from losing and regaining his throne three times. His son Frederick was also elected King of Poland (as Augustus III in 1734), over his rival Stanislaus Leczcynski, Louis XV's father-in-law. He too lost his throne twice, and twice regained it.

Germany: Prussia

W hen Napoleon abolished the Holy Roman Empire in 1806, observers thought it quite dead. However, they had failed to take into account a tenacious and ambitious family. Originally from Southern Germany, the Hohenzollerns had lived in relative obscurity until the fifteenth century, when they bought from the Emperor the northern province of Brandenburg and the title of Prince. Soon afterwards they acquired Prussia, previously cleared of the Lithuanians, her original inhabitants, who were exterminated by Teutonic knights. The Hohenzollerns held on to their nordic swamps, made of them a state, and founded a capital, Berlin.

In 1700 their efforts were rewarded with the title of King, granted by Emperor Leopold I for considerable remuneration. In the eighteenth century, under Frederick II the Great, Prussia annexed Silesia and parts of Poland and became a major European power. Later, as foreign minister, Bismarck defeated Austria in the Franco-Prussian War, unified Germany, resuscitated the German Empire, and offered it to the Hohenzollerns in 1871. This second Empire was to last only fifty-one years; it was swept away in the whirlwind of the First World War, which the Hohenzollerns were accused – probably falsely – of launching. In that short period, however, they had time enough to fashion modern Germany, an industrious, industrial and prosperous country.

The kings of Prussia established a fine collection of Crown Jewels. Decimated by the disastrous Napoleonic Wars, it was again filled out, with poetic justice, by the jewels seized from the coach Napoleon abandoned at Waterloo. The most historical pieces, which miraculously escaped the Russian troops in 1945, are exhibited in the Palace of Charlottenburg, near Berlin, which was restored after being bombed in the Second World War.

37 Royal Sceptre of Prussia. In 1701 the Holy Roman Emperor, Leopold I, in need of the armies of the Elector of Brandenburg for the coming war with France and having nothing tangible to offer him in exchange, invested him with the title of King, which his family had long coveted. However, it was not possible to transform a province of the Empire into a kingdom, for that would have been a slight to the majesty of the Emperor. Therefore one of the Elector's provinces outside the boundaries of the Empire was chosen for the purpose. This was Prussia, at the time largely wild and uninhabited. Delirious with happiness, Frederick I ran to Königsberg, the medieval seat of Prussia, to be crowned. He ordered magnificent instruments of coronation, of which the sceptre is the most elegant. A crowned eagle, the symbol of Prussia, is set with diamonds and holds in its centre a garnet that was a gift from Tsar Peter the Great to the new King of Prussia.

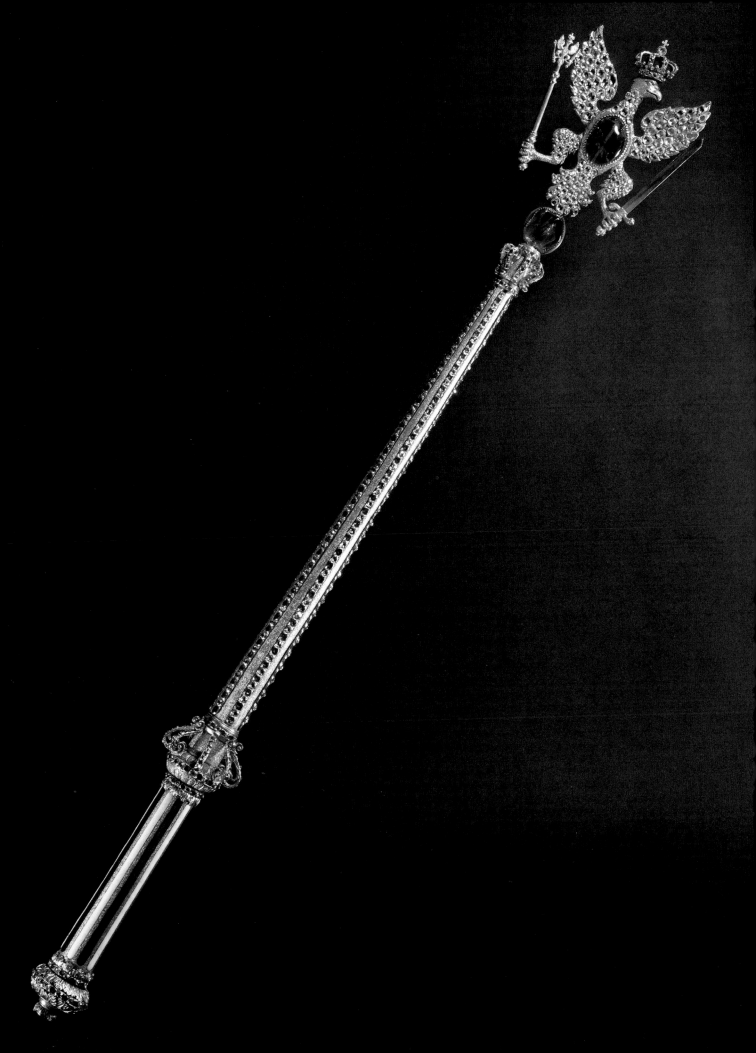

38 Snuffbox of Frederick the Great

Military genius, wily diplomat, distinguished composer and friend of Voltaire (who made fun of his attempts at versification), Frederick II the Great was the greatest king of Prussia, which he transformed into a European power. He was cold to his unfortunate wife, and gave her few jewels. Meanwhile, however, he assembled for himself an extraordinary collection of ornate snuffboxes, in gold and other precious materials, inlaid with gems in the shape of flowers. This one is in gold, inlaid with mother-of-pearl and precious stones.

39 Royal Crown of Prussia

This gold crown, inlaid with large diamonds and pearls, was ordered in 1889 by William II, Emperor of Germany and also King of Prussia, and fashioned along the lines of the crowns of his predecessors. It was never used, because the new emperors of Germany were not crowned, but William had himself photographed with it several times, in the haughty poses he liked to assume. A brilliant but insecure and easily influenced ruler, he created for himself the image of the warlike Kaiser; it had little basis in reality but, unfortunately for him, history believed and adhered to it. After his fall in 1918 the Hohenzollern dynasty, protected successively by the Weimar Republic, the Nazi regime and the Federal Republic, kept its Crown Jewels. The crown itself still belongs to the head of the family.

40 Emperor William I. In 1871 William I of Prussia, then seventy-four years old, became Emperor of Germany thanks to Bismarck and the Franco-Prussian War. Popular imagery represented him wearing an imaginary crown reminiscent of that of Charlemagne, the prestigious emperor to whom the new German Empire would have liked to hitch its destiny (see pl. 14).

41 The coronation of William I. In 1861, ten years before becoming Emperor of Germany, William I inherited the throne of Prussia; like his predecessors, he was crowned at Königsberg.

France

No European dynasty can rival the House of France in antiquity, distinction and continuity. After the elimination of Charlemagne's descendants, in 987, the great feudal lords of France chose for their king Hugh Capet, a man issued from an already illustrious family which owned a small province, the Duchy of France, centred around a modest city, Paris. They chose him precisely because he was the most unobtrusive and the poorest among them.

The House of France, descended from Hugh Capet, was to reign without interruption until 1792 and then from 1814 to 1848, almost a thousand years all told. Generation after generation of kings absorbed province after province with matchless tenacity, pushed back their neighbouring enemies, the English and later the Habsburgs, hobbled the ambitious and anarchical nobility, and literally 'made' France. Having fashioned a strong and centralized state, they threw themselves into absolutism, which was ultimately to cause their downfall. The shock of the Revolution of 1789 was such that even now France has not recovered her balance, having consumed, in a century and a half, four monarchies and five republics, with the help of three revolutions. Meanwhile, branches of the House of France had split off to reign over Spain, the Two Sicilies, the Latin Empire of Constantinople, Hungary, Portugal and Brazil.

In the fourteenth century Charles V, whose reign was a luminous intermission during the horror of the Hundred Years' War, assembled the first important collection of Crown Jewels. During the Renaissance the Valois, who were politically disasters but fine patrons, considerably enlarged it. But it was Louis XIV, through his massive buying, who made of it the first collection in Europe. It was completely annihilated by the Revolution of 1789. The jewels were smashed and melted down with revolutionary zeal, and the gems were stolen in a sensational burglary. Napoleon reconstituted the Crown Jewels with the little that could be recovered and a few additions. Napoleon III added

42 **Statue of Charles VI.** This precious object of gold, enamel and gems is one of the rare surviving examples of the rich and imaginative work of medieval goldsmiths. It was ordered in the late fourteenth century by Isabel of Bavaria for her husband Charles VI, King of France, who is shown kneeling, wearing a vest decorated with fleurs-de-lys. It was at the beginning of their marriage, when they were still deeply in love. Later, after Charles had gone mad and Isabel had plunged into a life of debauchery, she literally sold France to England at the Treaty of Troyes in 1420 and publicly admitted that her son the Dauphin, the future Charles VII, was illegitimate. Lost by a woman, the kingdom was soon to be regained by another – Joan of Arc.

more, and had quite a number reset. The collection had survived the Hundred Days (the period before Napoleon's final defeat at Waterloo), the revolutions of 1830 and 1848, and the destructive rage of the Commune, but it succumbed to the virtuous dogmatism of the Third Republic. For reasons that were more political than financial, that regime sold almost all the Crown Jewels in 1883. Only a few of the most famous gems and most historical jewels were kept. They are now exhibited in the Galerie d'Apollon at the Louvre in Paris.

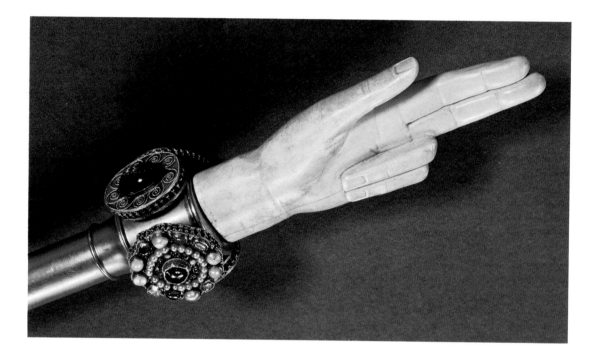

43 Hand of Justice

The Hand of Justice was an object peculiar to the coronation of French kings, symbolizing their judicial power. This particular one was made for the coronation of Napoleon in 1804. The precious stones at the base of the ivory hand were actually the setting of a ring from the Carolingian era. It was called the Ring of St Denis, after one of Paris's patron saints, who was decapitated on a hill that was later named after his martyrdom: Montmartre, Mont des Martyrs.

44 Order of St Michael

One of the greatest kings of France, Louis XI, whom history has falsely accused of many a sin, founded the Order of St Michael in the fifteenth century, as a mark of his devotion to France's protecting archangel. During the Renaissance the Valois kings made of this decoration a distinguished jewel. This one was carved by one of the greatest goldsmiths of all time, Benvenuto Cellini, and now belongs to the head of the House of France, Henry Count of Paris.

45 Parure of sapphires and diamonds of Queen Marie Antoinette

This superb set of jewels belonged to Queen Marie Antoinette. After vanishing during the Revolution it mysteriously reappeared to be bought by Napoleon, who gave it to his wife, the future Empress Josephine. At her death it went to her daughter Queen Hortense. Ruined by the fall of the Bonapartes, Hortense sold it to Louis-Philippe, then Duke of Orleans. Since then it has been worn by the wives of the successive heads of the House of France and now belongs to the present pretender to the throne, the Count of Paris. It is unique in that it has passed through the hands of three dynasties that ruled France: the Bourbons, the Bonapartes and the Orleans.

46 The Duchess of Guise, Isabelle of France, great-granddaughter of King Louis-Philippe, married her first cousin the Duke of Guise, the head of the House of France. She died in 1961. In this photograph she wears Marie Antoinette's parure of sapphires and diamonds.

47 The Countess of Paris, Isabelle of Orleans-Braganza belongs to the branch of the House of France that became the Imperial family of Brazil. She married her cousin Henry Count of Paris, the current pretender to the throne of France. Like her mother-in-law in the preceding photograph, she is wearing Marie Antoinette's parure.

48 The Regent Diamond

This 140-carat diamond is one of the purest and brightest in the world. It was found in the eighteenth century by a slave in a mine of central India. He hid the diamond in a bandage wrapped around a self-inflicted wound on his leg, and then managed to escape and make his way to the coast. There he met the captain of a British ship, to whom he offered half the price of the diamond in exchange for passage to a free country. Once at sea temptation proved too strong for the captain, who killed the slave and tossed his body overboard. He sold the diamond to an Indian merchant in Bombay for 5000 dollars. The merchant then sold it to William Pitt, who at the time was governor of Madras. When Pitt returned to England he decided to sell, but no one could afford the diamond. However, the Duke of Orleans, Regent of France, was ready to pay any price for an alliance with England; he paid two-and-a-half million pounds for the gem, which was thenceforth known after him as the Regent.

The Regent disappeared with the other diamonds of the Crown in the robbery of 1792 (see Introduction), and later was found hidden behind a beam in an attic. Napoleon had it set in the hilt of the sword he wore at his coronation. In 1814,

as the Allied troops advanced on Paris, his wife Empress Marie Louise escaped from the capital with the Crown Jewels. She was in constant danger of being stopped and searched, or robbed by marauding Cossacks. The coronation sword was too long to hide under her clothes with the other jewels. One of her faithful courtiers, Monsieur de Meneval, broke the sword and hid the hilt under his coat. Cossacks eventually did stop the carriage, but they found no jewels, since they dared not search the august personalities inside. By order of Napoleon the Regent was returned to the provisional government and reinstated in the treasures of the Crown. When the Second Empire fell in 1870, the triumphant Commune sent representatives to the Bank of France with orders to hand over the Crown Jewels, including the Regent. However, the communards' threats of violence met with no success. For, shortly before the empire crumbled, the diamonds and the Regent had been removed in an iron box marked 'special projectiles' and sent from Paris to Brest, where the box stayed on a ship, waiting to sail if the situation grew worse. The Commune was crushed in May 1871, and the Regent went back to the Louvre.

49 Diadem of emeralds and diamonds

Having assumed the title of Emperor in May 1804 Napoleon I assembled a splendid set of Crown Jewels by adding massive purchases to those gems of the kings of France that had survived the Revolution. This diadem set with large emeralds is one of the jewels in which he smothered his second wife Archduchess Marie Louise of Austria, 'Imperial heifer sacrificed to the Minotaur'. 'She is entirely satisfactory', Napoleon announced to his courtiers after their wedding-night in April 1810. After Napoleon's death Marie Louise married a one-eyed hero, Count Neipperg, in whose arms she had already found consolation after the fall of her imperial husband.

50 The Sancy Diamond

This 55-carat diamond was bought in Constantinople in the sixteenth century by Nicolas de Sancy, the French Ambassador to Turkey. Later he became Minister of Finance under Henry IV, who was always short of funds and begged Sancy to mortgage the diamond at a Swiss bank. Accordingly Sancy sent the stone to Switzerland in the care of a faithful servant. On his way, at Saulieu, the servant was attacked, robbed and killed. Sancy was desperate at having lost the servant and the diamond, but he nevertheless had his doubts; he knew the servant well, and could not imagine the man letting himself be robbed of the stone. Sancy had the body disinterred and dissected. The diamond was found inside the corpse's stomach. The servant had swallowed it rather than let the bandits take it.

Sancy later sold the diamond to James I of England, and thus it became part of the jewels of the British Crown. When Charles I, the son of James I, was defeated by Oliver Cromwell, his wife Queen Henrietta Maria, the daughter of Henry IV, went into exile in her native France, taking with her the Sancy and other diamonds. Ruined, without enough money even to buy wood for her fire, she sold the diamond. It was bought by the French prime minister, Cardinal Mazarin, who was mad about precious stones. At his death, in order to secure forgiveness for his enormous embezzlements, he left the gem and other diamonds to Louis XIV.

Now part of the Crown Jewels of France, it was stolen with the other diamonds of the Crown in the burglary of 1792 and disappeared for several years. After the Revolution it reappeared in the collections of Prince Demidov, an eccentric and cruel Russian millionaire. No one ever learned where or how he had acquired it. Many years later the Sancy was bought by a Maharaja and taken to India. The Maharaja was crushed to death by one of his own elephants, and his tearful widows sold the Sancy to the first Lord Astor. In 1978 his grandson negotiated its sale with the then President Valery Giscard d'Estaing of France. The diamond arrived in Paris, to be received by members of the government, like an important political figure, and returned to the Louvre after an absence of a hundred and fifty years.

51 The Mancini Pearls

'I leave, you cry, and you are the master', said Marie Mancini to her lover, Louis XIV, when he separated from her. He was still in love with her but, under pressure from his entourage, he had been forced to abandon the idea of marrying her. In remembrance of their idyll she kept these two pearls mounted as earrings.

The pearls had once been part of the fabulous collections of the Medici and were brought to France by Marie de Medici when she married Henry IV in 1600. A fat and stupid queen, she always smothered herself in pearls. Her earrings were passed on to her daughter Henrietta Maria who became Queen of England when she married Charles I. They returned to France during her exile, where she sold them to her nephew Louis XIV, who hastened to give them to Marie Mancini.

When Louis abandoned Marie she retired to Italy, married Prince Colonna, and lived a miserable, tormented life. Of all Louis XIV's mistresses she was certainly the most ardently loved. 'Pulvus et ceneris' – dust and ashes – was the epitaph chosen by her son for the gravestone of that flamboyant lady.

52 Clasp of St Louis

According to legend this clasp of gold, enamel and gems belonged in the thirteenth century to Louis IX, who was known as the saint king. Certainly it was part of the inventory of Charles V a hundred years later, and from then on was used to fasten the mantle the kings wore at their coronation. It is decorated with fleurs-de-lys, a very ancient symbol that was adopted by the kings of France after the twelfth century.

53 Joyeuse, the sword of Charlemagne
54 Sword of Charles X

The sword known as Joyeuse, which was said to have belonged to Charlemagne, in fact dates back to the eleventh or twelfth century. Used at the coronation of all the kings of France, it miraculously survived the Revolution to serve in the coronation of the last king, Charles X, in 1824. For the ceremony he also had a lighter one made, inlaid with 1576 diamonds chosen from the gems of the Crown. A few years ago daring burglars stole it, in daylight, from the Galerie d'Apollon at the Louvre. It has never been found.

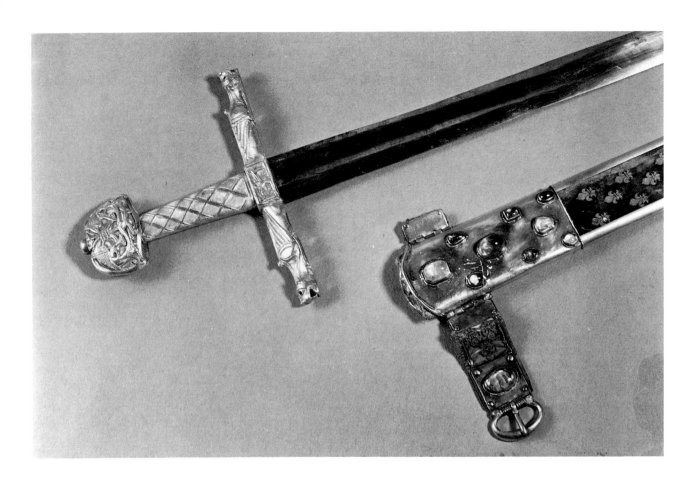

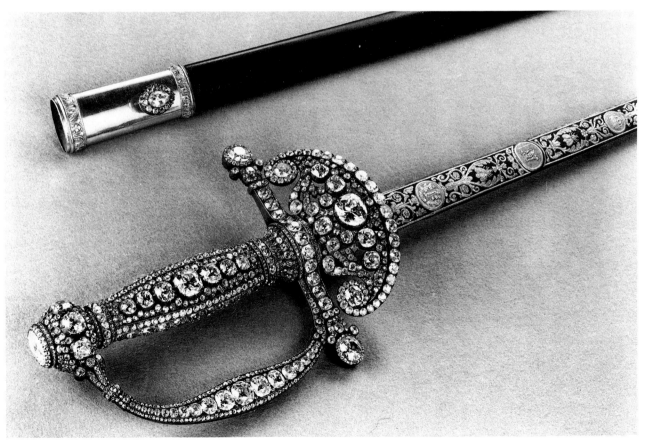

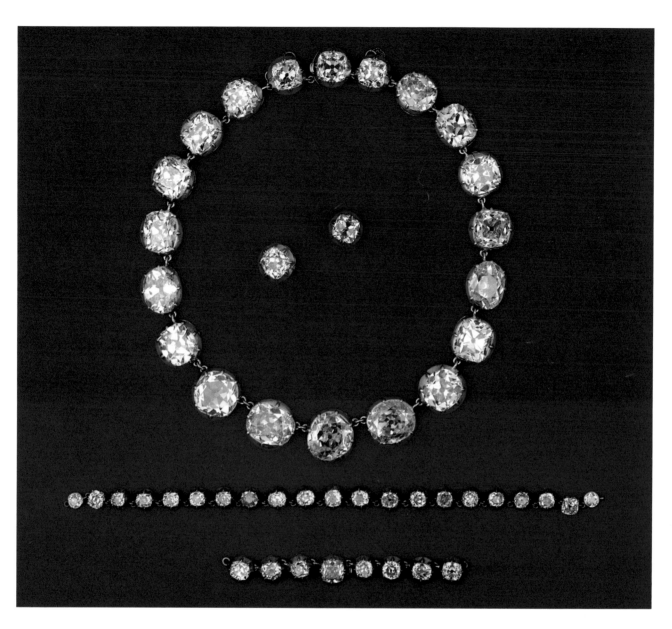

55 Necklace made with the diamonds of 'the Queen's necklace'
56 Model of 'the Queen's necklace'

This jewel, which did not belong to the Crown of France, sparked the loudest scandal of the eighteenth century. In 1785 the Comtesse de la Motte, an adventuress, had the necklace, the most expensive jewel of the era, delivered to her. She in turn was supposed to take it to Marie Antoinette, but she stole it instead. Her (perhaps unwilling) accomplice, Prince Louis de Rohan, Cardinal and Head Chaplain of France, was arrested in the Château of Versailles, as he left a mass he had just led. Another accomplice, the shady magus Cagliostro, was also imprisoned. Comtesse de la Motte was publicly whipped and branded on the shoulder with a fleur-de-lys, symbol of royal justice. Her trial compromised Marie Antoinette, although the latter was clearly innocent. Comtesse de la Motte escaped from prison, took refuge in London, and sold the diamonds she had removed from the necklace. She died there in 1791; but there is a theory that she lived for a long time under an assumed name in Odessa, enjoying the secret protection of the Tsar. Twenty-two of the large diamonds she sold in London were mounted in a new necklace, now in a private collection.

57 The Hope Diamond

This beautiful blue diamond weighing 44.5 carats, the largest diamond of that colour in the world, is what remains of the French Blue, one of the most famous gems of the Crown of France, worn in a decoration by several kings. Stolen in the burglary of 1792, it was recut and passed from hand to hand (one owner was Sultan Abdul Hamid II of Turkey) until the jeweller Harry Winston gave it to the Smithsonian Institution. Legend holds that the stone was originally the eye of a Hindu idol, and was plucked out by robbers. Moreover it is considered one of the most evil stones in the world. A dozen violent deaths and disasters in two royal families are linked to possession of the Hope Diamond and have upheld that reputation.

Great Britain: England

The English throne has been occupied by Welsh and Scottish but never by English kings. The present royal family, successor to Anglo-Saxon, Norman, Angevin, Scottish and German dynasties, is nevertheless the supreme incarnation of England.

There are a few relics left from the pre-Norman Conquest Anglo-Saxon kings, but almost nothing remains from the Tudors and Plantagenets, for the puritanical vandalism of Oliver Cromwell's regime in the mid-seventeenth century decreed that all the Crown Jewels be melted down. When the Stuarts returned to the throne in 1660 they reconstituted the Crown Jewels as well as they could. The first Hanoverians added little. It was not until the splendid spendthrift George IV came to the throne in 1820 that a profusion of gems enriched the royal treasure. Then, as the empire extended, a stream of precious stones began to flow from the colonies.

The Tower of London holds a few pieces from the post-Restoration Stuarts and the Hanoverians, although many of them have been reset or otherwise altered. Most of the instruments of coronation on display there have been made in the twentieth century and are not distinguished by their elegance. Nevertheless, they are set with many admirable gems which are themselves very old and laden with history. The royal palaces shelter many of the actual jewels of the Crown, and the Queen keeps in her coffers her collection – which is never exhibited – of 'private' jewels, which is probably the most sumptuous in the whole of Europe.

58 Imperial State Crown: detail showing the Black Prince's Ruby (top) and the Cullinan Diamond.

59 Imperial State Crown·

The Imperial State Crown fashioned for the coronation of Elizabeth II in 1953 was built on the model of the crown of Queen Victoria. It replaced the Crown of St Edward on the head of the ruler immediately after the coronation. Though modern in design, it is set with very ancient gems.

The Black Prince's Ruby (pl. 58), in fact a spinel, is set in the central panel of the Imperial State Crown. In the fourteenth century, Castille was ruled by the terrible and aptly named king, Peter the Cruel. One day, one of the Arab chieftains who still ruled Spain, Abu Said, came to surrender. Peter welcomed him affably, having heard that Abu Said had with him jewels of great value, including a matchless ruby; he invited the chieftain to dinner, and during the banquet had his servants killed while he personally stabbed Abu Said to death. The famous ruby was found on the corpse.

When his subjects and his illegitimate brother rebelled against him Peter called England to his aid in the person of the Black Prince, whom he then rewarded with Abu Said's ruby. Thenceforth part of the Crown Jewels of England, it was worn by Henry V on his helmet when he crushed the French forces at Agincourt in 1415. Later Richard III also wore the ruby on his helmet, at the Battle of Bosworth, where he lost his throne and his life. Under Oliver Cromwell the Puritans melted, destroyed and dispersed the Crown Jewels. The Black Prince's Ruby was bought by a jeweller who resold it to Charles II after the Restoration of the Stuarts in 1660.

The Cullinan Diamond (pl. 58) decorates the brow of the Imperial State Crown, just below the Black Prince's Ruby. One afternoon in 1905, Mr Wells, the superintendent of the Premier diamond mine in South Africa, was making his usual tour of the mine when his eye was caught by a sparkling object, lit by the rays of the sun, encrusted in the earth wall a foot away. He managed to pry the object out. It could not be a diamond, for there was no diamond of that size on earth; it had to be glass. Nevertheless, his professional conscience led him to have it analysed, and the piece of glass proved to be a diamond weighing 3601 carats, the largest ever found. It was named after Sir Thomas Cullinan, who had opened the Premier Mine and happened to be touring it that day. Later the Transvaal government made a gift of the monstrous stone to the King of England, Edward VII, who had it cut in several pieces. The largest, Cullinan One, known as the Star of Africa, was set in the King's sceptre, while the next-to-largest (319 carats), the Cullinan Two, was mounted in the Imperial State Crown.

St Edward's Sapphire is set in the centre of the cross that stands atop the Imperial State Crown. According to legend Edward the Confessor wore it on a ring. On his way one day to the consecration of a chapel, he was accosted by a beggar. Since he had already given away all his money in alms he slipped the ring off his finger and gave it to the beggar. Many years later two pilgrims fresh from the Holy Land returned the ring, which had been handed to them by an old man with instructions to bring it to England. They said that he had claimed to be St John, and had told them that, a long time before, in the guise of a beggar, he had received the ring from the hands of the king. He congratulated the king on his generosity and promised that they would soon meet again in paradise. Edward died soon afterward, in 1066, and was buried with the recovered ring on his finger. When his coffin was opened two hundred years later, his body was found in a state of perfect preservation. The Abbot of Westminster slipped the sapphire off his finger. It has been part of the Crown Jewels of England ever since.

60 King Alfred's Jewel

Alfred the Great, the most famous of the pre-Norman Conquest Anglo-Saxon kings, attempted to halt the Danish invasion of England. Temporarily beaten in 878, he was forced to hide in the marshes of Somerset where, according to legend, he lost this jewel of filigreed gold, enamel and rock crystal. It was later found by chance. Both its shape and its purpose are a mystery. Inscribed on it in Celtic are the words 'Alfred had me made'.

Disguised as a bard, Alfred slipped into the Danish camp and gathered information which later enabled him to defeat his fearsome enemies. In 886 he retook London and reunified England. After saving his country he devoted the rest of his reign to developing its civilization and its laws.

61 Coronation Throne

This thirteenth-century chair contains in its base the Stone of Scone, a legendary relic. It is said the stone was the pillow on which Jacob slept when he had his dream. It was taken to the Temple of Jerusalem, to be used in the coronation of the kings of Judaea. In the fourth century BC the daughter of the last of these kings took it on her travels through Egypt and Spain to Ireland. There she married an Irish prince, and in later centuries the kings of Ireland were crowned on the stone. In the early Middle Ages the Irish invaded Scotland, and one of their princes became the Scottish king. The stone was kept at Scone, the capital, where it served in the coronations of thirty-four kings of Scotland. In 1296 it was the King of England, Edward I, who invaded Scotland. He seized the stone, brought it to London, and had it set in a throne built for it. Since then all the kings of England (and Britain) have been crowned on that throne and on the stone.

62 Sceptres

From left to right

The King's Sceptre with the Cross dates back to the Restoration of the Stuarts in 1660, but its head was changed when Edward VII inserted in it the largest cut diamond in the world, the 530-carat Star of Africa, a fragment of the Cullinan Diamond.

The King's Sceptre with the Dove was also made in the reign of Charles II, but imitates a model introduced under the Tudors.

The Queen's Sceptre with the Cross, made of gold and crystal, was ordered for the coronation in 1685 of Mary of Modena, the second wife of James II.

The Queen's Ivory Rod, a sceptre of gold and ivory, was also made for Mary of Modena.

63 The Pendant of Naseby

Charles I, a brave but narrow-minded man, had the charm of the Stuarts, but lacked his father's political sense. His subjects' exasperation and anger – at his financial expedients, eleven-year 'personal rule' and associations with 'popery' – eventually led them to rebel. His last defeat in the Civil War, against Oliver Cromwell's troops at Naseby in 1645, was fatal to his cause. He lost all hope of recovering his throne, and also this jewel, which had adorned his hat.

64 Small Diamond Crown of Queen Victoria

This crown, whose lightness and elegance contrast with the other British crowns, was ordered by Queen Victoria for her personal use. She found the Imperial State Crown too heavy, and resented the complicated procedures involved in removing it from the Tower of London when needed.

65 Queen Victoria at one of the jubilees of her sixty-four-year reign, wearing the small diamond crown shown below.

66 Indian Armlet of Ranjit Singh, with replica of the Koh-i-Noor Diamond

In the eighteenth century the ruler of Persia, Nadir Shah, invaded India, took Delhi, seized the treasures of the Indian capital and took prisoner Mohammed Shah, the Great Mogul. A spy-slave informed Nadir Shah that the Great Mogul had hidden in his turban his greatest treasure, a diamond of matchless beauty. Nadir Shah invited his prisoner to dinner and, after the meal, suggested that as a gesture of friendship they exchange turbans. Pale, terrified and ashamed of being discovered, the Great Mogul had no choice but to comply. Nadir Shah returned to his quarters, feverishly unwrapped the turban, and found a magnificent diamond shining on the cloth. 'Koh-i-Noor!' he exclaimed – 'A mountain of light'.

Nadir Shah returned to Persia with his trophy, but he was assassinated soon afterward. His son and heir was toppled by a rebellion. Arrested, tortured, blinded by his enemies, he refused to divulge the Koh-i-Noor's hiding-place. When the King of Afghanistan came to his rescue, the dying son of Nadir Shah, soaked in his own blood, handed him the Koh-i-Noor.

The King took it back to Afghanistan. Years later his grandson, Zaman, was deposed, imprisoned and blinded by his own brother, but managed to hide the Koh-i-Noor under the floor of his cell. Eventually he escaped with the gem and took refuge at Lahore. There in 1813 he was received by Ranjit Singh, the Lion of the Punjab, who treated him with great respect but insisted that he give up the Koh-i-Noor. Singh had the diamond set in the armlet shown here. Later, when he failed in his rebellion against the British, one of the conditions of the peace treaty was the delivery of the gem. It was presented to Queen Victoria. Since then the diamond has adorned the crown of the queen consort, for it has the reputation of bringing luck to women and misfortune to men.

67 **Queen Alexandra** on the day of her coronation, 9 August 1901, after her husband Edward VII had succeeded to the throne on the death of his mother, Queen Victoria. In the centre of her crown is the Koh-i-Noor Diamond.

68 Crown of Queen Elizabeth the Queen Mother

This crown was executed in 1937 to serve in the coronation of Queen Consort Elizabeth, the wife of George VI. In the centre it holds the famous Koh-i-Noor diamond, worn before in a crown by Queen Alexandra of Denmark. This diamond, which once weighed 186 carats (see replica, pl. 66) was recut in 1851 to give it more regularity and sparkle. In its present form it weighs only 109 carats.

69 St Edward's Crown

The 'real' Crown of St Edward (in fact made some two hundred years after his death), which had served in the coronation of the kings of England from Edward II to Charles I, was melted down during Oliver Cromwell's rule. This one is a vague copy made after the Restoration. George V replaced the fake gems of the crown with precious and semi-precious stones. Traditionally it is with this, the least precious of all the crowns in the Tower of London, that the ruler is crowned.

Great Britain: Scotland

*S*cotland, whose very ancient historical beginnings remain obscure, made her first appearance as a coherent kingdom in the ninth century under Kenneth I McAlpine. The descendants of his dynasty include such famous historical figures as Duncan and Macbeth. Dominated by wars with England, the history of Scotland is a romantic tapestry of acts of great heroism and great brutality.

The Stewarts came to the throne with Robert II in the fourteenth century. Although engaging and often seductive in their storybook quality, they were for the most part markedly incompetent, and perpetuated the Scottish tradition of assassinated kings. No country has endured so many violent deaths among its rulers. This long and bloody tragedy was, however, to end as peacefully as could be, when in 1603 the King of Scotland James VI inherited the throne of England as James I from his cousin Elizabeth I. After centuries of quarrels and warfare, the two kingdoms were united under the same sceptre.

Although most of the Crown Jewels were stolen or sold over the centuries, the Scottish instruments of coronation escaped foreign wars and civil wars. After having been carried away, hidden and taken out again several times, after having once lain locked up in a safe for more than a hundred years, these superb examples of Renaissance jewellery rest quietly, under the gaze of visitors, in Edinburgh Castle.

70 **The Darnley Jewel.** Following the fashion of the Renaissance, this jewel is covered with mottoes, emblems and mysterious symbols. It was ordered by Margaret Douglas, the wife of the Regent of Scotland, Matthew Stewart, Earl of Lennox. An energetic, ambitious woman, she did her utmost to further the advancement of her family, and in 1565 secured the marriage of her son, Lord Darnley, to his cousin, Mary Queen of Scots. Margaret saw her beloved grandson don the crown of Scotland as James VI, but she died before he inherited the Crown of England. This jewel now belongs to James's descendant, Elizabeth II.

71 Royal Crown of Scotland

This crown, which is far more elegant than the English crowns, was ordered in the sixteenth century by James V. It incorporated the far older crown of his Stewart ancestors, as well, so he claimed, as material from the crown of his glorious predecessor, Robert Bruce. King at seventeen months of age, James died before he was thirty. He was told of the birth of his daughter on his death bed. Mary Queen of Scots, a queen from birth, was crowned when she was nine months old. One may assume the crown served only in a symbolic capacity at the coronation. It was used by her son James I and her grandson Charles I. In modern times the crown is merely presented to British rulers to signify their accession.

72 Elizabeth II returning the Crown of Scotland into the care of the Duke of Hamilton after a thanksgiving service in Edinburgh, 24 June 1953.

73 Ruby Ring of Charles I with Royal Orders

According to tradition, this ring set with a flat ruby was the coronation ring of Charles I. The last Stuart, Cardinal York, who died in 1807, bequeathed it – along with other crown jewels which had been carried off by James II in 1688 – to George II of Britain. With it are the insignia of the Order of the Garter, left in the treasures of Scotland by the King of Britain, William IV, as well as those of the Order of the Thistle. The latter, one of the oldest and most venerable in Europe, has remained the Scottish Order par excellence. This eighteenth-century jewel conceals a miniature of Clementina Sobieski, the wife of the Old Pretender James Stuart, son of James II.

Northern Europe: Sweden

The origins of the Kingdom of Sweden are lost in the mists of ancient legends. The first kings, Vikings, were probably slightly piratical. After a long era of troubles and confusion there emerged a national dynasty, the Vasa, who produced several exceptional men a few generations later. Its founder, Gustavus Vasa, expelled the Danish occupiers in 1523, was elected king as Gustavus I, and restored Sweden's unity and greatness. His grandson, Gustavus II Adolphus, the greatest king of Sweden, was the hero of the seventeenth century and the victor of the Thirty Years' War, in which he lost his life.

Queen Christina, a woman of phenomenal intelligence, culture and eccentricity, succeeded her father Gustavus II in 1632 and amazed her era by her extravagance. Later came the brief reigns of various foreign dynasties, including a few lightning-bolts. Charles XII, a mysterious genius and brilliant general, shot across the skies of the eighteenth century like a meteor; and Gustavus III, an inspired patron, turned his court into a haven of civilization in imitation of Versailles before dying in a fantastic assassination. In 1810 a Gascon soldier risen from the ranks, Marshal Bernadotte, Napoleon's companion and rival, was chosen to be Crown Prince of Sweden after a series of incredible misunderstandings. He became king as Charles XIV in 1818, and gained a reputation of being wise and shrewd. His descendants still reign, more Swedish than the Swedes, even in appearance.

The Vasa kings and their immediate successors assembled the most complete set of instruments of coronation in Europe, which are exhibited in the Royal Palace in Stockholm, with a unique and sumptuous set of funereal crowns, destined to be placed on or inside the tombs of kings and queens. The actual Crown Jewels are many and superb, but they remain the private property of the royal family.

74 **Sword of Gustavus III.** This elegant sword, richly inlaid with precious stones, recalls the sumptuous reign of Gustavus III, who ordered it for his coronation in 1771. Horrified by the French Revolution, he tried, with his friend Axel of Fersen, to save Louis XVI and Marie Antoinette. Part of the nobility, weary of his absolutist ways, hatched a conspiracy against him. At a masked ball one night in 1792 Count Ankarström shot the disguised king at point-blank range. He died of his wounds fourteen days later.

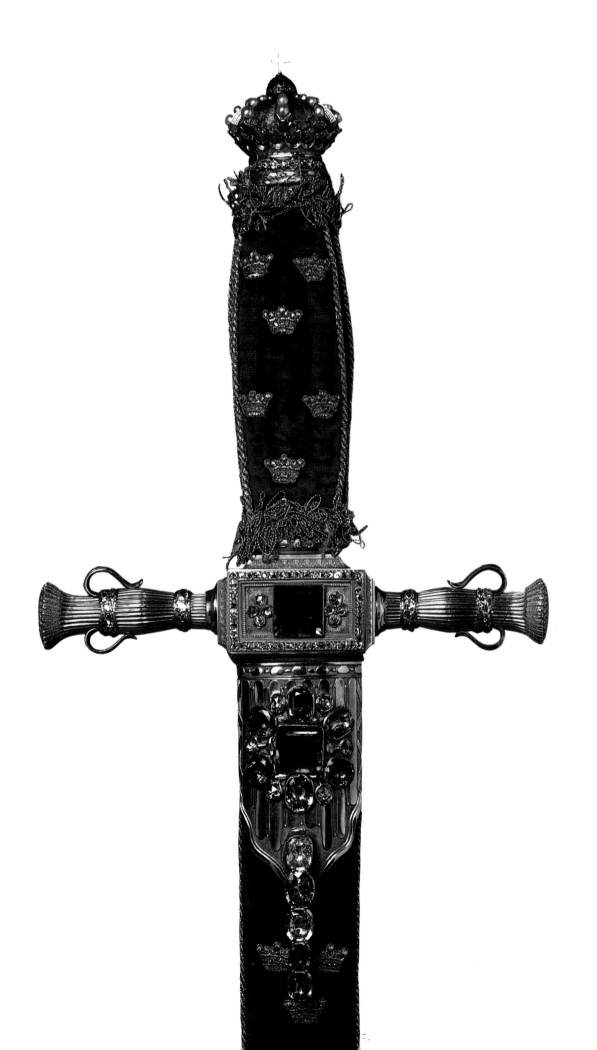

75 Silver Throne
76 Crown of Queen Maria Eleonora

Queen Christina of Sweden, daughter and heiress of the great Gustavus Adolphus, wanted to lend exceptional sparkle to her coronation in 1650. She was given this silver throne, which has been used by all her successors. She was crowned with the crown of her mother, Maria Eleonora of Brandenburg, which she had modified for the occasion, and which has since been the crown of the queen consorts of Sweden.

Queen Christina was considered a natural phenomenon. She became queen at the age of six in 1632, when her father died. At eight she spoke Latin and Ancient Greek fluently. At twelve she was corresponding with Descartes. At eighteen she dismissed her regents and began to reign on her own. Ten years later, in 1654, weary of power, she abdicated, despite the pleas of her subjects, and left Sweden. She stupefied the French Court, had her lover Monaldeschi assassinated at Fontainebleau, and converted to Catholicism in order to visit Italy. She settled in Rome, where she spent the last thirty-five years of her life. This extraordinary queen is one of the only two women ever to be buried in the Basilica of St Peter.

77 Crown of the Hereditary Prince

When she abdicated, the unmarried Queen Christina left her crown to her cousin, who became Charles X Gustavus. As Hereditary Prince at Christina's coronation, he had worn this crown of very special shape, ordered for the occasion. It has remained the emblem of the heir to the Swedish throne.

78, 79 Orb and Crown of Eric XIV

Eric XIV was the eldest son and successor of Gustavus Vasa, the founder of the dynasty. When he came to the throne in 1560 Eric decided that his coronation would be remembered, and had foreign courts investigated to discover the different rituals of the ceremony. He also ordered a new set of instruments of coronation for the occasion; the most famous and most beautiful among them is this crown. On its base Eric had lions carved in the enamel, representing his other kingdom of Norway, as well as leopards which are the symbol of Denmark – a gesture prompted by his inability to forgive the kings of Denmark for having kept on their coat-of-arms the three crowns emblematic of Sweden. Eric's successor, his brother John III, had Eric's monogram on the floweret replaced by pearls.

The orb was also ordered by Eric XIV. A unique object, it bears a map of the world and recalls his advanced knowledge of geography.

His reign was disastrous. He engaged in unsuccessful wars and, aspiring to absolutism, ordered many arbitrary executions, so much so that he soon came to be detested. His two brothers, seeing their liberty and their lives threatened, rebelled against him; he was deposed in 1569 and thrown in a dungeon, where he consoled himself with music and the composition of psalms. In 1577 he was poisoned, probably on the order of one of his brothers.

Since then the crown has served all the kings of Sweden at their coronation; since the abolition of that ceremony it has served at the enthronement, including that of the present king, Charles Gustavus.

80 Louise of Battenberg, the sister of Lord Louis Mountbatten and the wife of Gustavus VI Adolphus of Sweden. In this photograph she is wearing a parure of

tourmalines and diamonds. It once belonged to the Beauharnais, the family into which Empress Josephine married in 1779 and from whom the Swedish dynasty is descended.

81 The future king Gustavus V, wearing the Crown of the Hereditary Prince. Born in 1858, Gustavus V was the godson of his great-grandmother Désirée Clary, Queen of Sweden, who had once been engaged to Napoleon. He was king from 1907 until 1950, the longest reign in Swedish history.

Northern Europe: Norway

Norway's early history was dominated by the Vikings. Local chieftains were not subjected to a single ruler until the tenth century. The names by which her kings were known – 'The Severe', 'The Bad', 'The Bloody Axe', 'The Barefoot', 'The Blind' – testify to an agitated history. When the last local dynasty died out in the fourteenth century the kingdom became the property of the kings of Denmark, who were forced to cede it to Sweden in 1814. By the twentieth century, however, the Norwegians, politely but firmly, showed the Swedes the door. Their independence recovered in 1905, they chose for their king none other than a Danish prince. He became Haakon VII and is father of the present king, Olaf V.

The instruments of coronation of Haakon VII and Queen Maud are kept in the Norge Bank in the ancient city of Trondheim.

82 King's crown, sword, orb, sceptre and ampulla. Having separated from Sweden in 1905, Norway exhibited its instruments of coronation, the symbols of its recovered independence. Ironically, they had been made for a King of Sweden, Charles XIV, formerly a Marshal of the Empire under Napoleon, Jean Bernadotte. For his coronation as King of Norway he ordered this crown, set with an enormous Brazilian amethyst, and this sceptre. As for the sword, it is the very one Bernadotte carried at the Battle of Leipzig, also known as the Battle of Nations, in 1813, when as an ally of Europe he contributed to the defeat of his former companion Napoleon.

83 Haakon VII and Queen Maud, the daughter of Edward VII of England, on the day of their coronation in 1905.

Northern Europe: Denmark

*T*he history of Denmark, considered the oldest kingdom in Europe, has been highly tumultuous. Her rulers have included saints, conquerors of England and a remarkable woman, Margaret I, who managed to unite all Scandinavia under her sceptre in the fourteenth century. Her dynasty died out soon after and was replaced by the ancient House of Oldenburg, which still reigns. Under various names several of its branches have occupied or still occupy the thrones of Russia, England, Greece, Sweden and Norway.

Considerably reduced from her former glory, Denmark is now a model of Parliamentary monarchy having been a model of Royal absolutism. She is ruled by a dynasty which, after enduring a number of scandals in the seventeenth and eighteenth centuries, has become a model of respectability and tranquillity under Margaret II.

Unhappy warriors or fearsome conquerors, inquiring minds or heroes of romantic dramas, the Oldenburg kings of Denmark, cultured patrons to a man, accumulated between the Renaissance and the nineteenth century a splendid collection of Crown Jewels and precious objects. Their treasure, the richest in Northern Europe, is exhibited in the cellars of Rosenborg Castle.

84 Royal Throne with Unicorns. This throne, ordered in the seventeenth century by Frederick III, the instigator of absolute monarchy in Denmark, was meant to recall those of the Scandinavian chieftains of earlier times. It is made of narwhal horn, which at the time was thought to be unicorn horn. Taking his inspiration from biblical descriptions of the throne of Solomon, Frederick had three life-sized silver lions (of which two are visible in this photograph) placed in front of it. In his own words, these animals were to 'display their fiery spirit and yet tremble before the throne'.

85 Crown of Christian IV

The longest reign in Danish history, lasting from 1588 to 1648, was that of the likeable and energetic Christian IV. Though marked by disastrous wars, it was also among the most beneficial of reigns, thanks to the King's administrative wisdom and his remarkable reforms. Christian IV kept a close watch over the design and execution of this crown of gold, enamels, pearls and precious stones. It is a masterpiece of sixteenth-century jewellery. Ruined by the Thirty Years' War, he was forced, to his deep regret, to pawn it.

86 Order of the Elephant

This decoration, which belonged to Christian IV, combines the Order of the Mailed Arm, which he founded, with the Order of the Elephant, founded by his ancestor Christian I in 1462. The latter is a good example of the symbolism that enjoyed such a vogue in the Middle Ages. The choice of this particular animal, however, is a mystery. Was it meant to recall some now-forgotten link between Denmark and the Orient? Or was it a symbol of strength or of wisdom? It is one of the most sought-after orders of knighthood in Europe.

87 Ampulla

When the Danish monarchy became absolute and hereditary under Frederick III in 1660, unction with Chrism was introduced into the coronation ceremony. This box of gold and enamel was designed to hold the sacred oil. In fact it looks more as if it belonged on the dressing-table of an elegant queen.

88 Sceptre of Frederick III

In order to symbolize the absolute monarchy he had secured for himself, Frederick III ordered new instruments of coronation. The most beautiful, the most poetic among them, is this sceptre adorned with a large enamel lily.

89 Bracelet, Necklace and Brooch of Diamonds, Rubies and Pearls

Sophia Magdalena of Brandenburg, the wife of Christian VI, bequeathed these jewels of rubies, diamonds and pearls to the Crown. Since then they have remained at the disposal of the ruling sovereign to be worn by his wife. The pearls of the necklace, which come from Scotland, are older than the others.

90 Ingrid of Sweden, the widow of Frederick IX and current Queen Mother of Denmark. She is wearing a parure of rubies and diamonds inherited from her ancestor Désirée Clary, Queen of Sweden. It was given to Désirée as a wedding present by a former fiancé who had bolted – Napoleon Bonaparte.

91 Margaret II, Queen of Denmark, photographed shortly after she came to the throne in 1972. The pearl and diamond necklace and the earrings she inherited from the royal family of Holland. The matching diadem was a gift from the Khedive of Egypt to Louise of Sweden, Queen of Denmark, the great-grandmother of Margaret II.

Northern Europe: Holland

Acounty of the Holy Roman Empire from the twelfth century, Holland came under Burgundy in the fifteenth century, and then, in 1500, under the Habsburgs. In 1568 the Dutch rebelled against the heavy Spanish yoke. The soul of the Revolt of the Netherlands was a prince of the House of Orange, William the Silent, who was neither Dutch nor Orange but a German Nassau. The father of the young republic, he was only its stadholder, the chief magistrate. He made the position hereditary within his family. One of his descendants, William III of Orange, a man worthy of his ancestor and namesake, in 1688 became King of England and Scotland.

In 1806 Napoleon made of occupied Holland a kingdom for his brother Louis. After Napoleon's fall the Dutch welcomed with enthusiasm the return of their stadholder, who had been expelled by the French. He proclaimed himself King of Holland under the title William I and in 1814 the Kingdom of the Netherlands was formed. He ordered instruments of coronation neither very valuable nor beautiful, more or less symbolic – there never was a coronation – and fitting to Holland's status as a republican monarchy. His son William II ordered a new set, only slightly more luxurious, which was used at the accession of the current queen, Beatrix.

The poverty of the 'Crown Jewels of Holland' only emphasizes the beauty of the private jewels of the royal family, one of the richest collections in Europe, most of it inherited from a Russian ancestor, Queen Anna Pavlovna, wife of William II.

92 Orb and Sword of William II. Made in silver gilt and set with imitation stones, they have been – with the Crown and Sceptre – used at the accession of each Dutch sovereign from William II until the present queen, Beatrix.

93 Crown and Sceptre of William II

In 1840, after William I had lost Belgium, by now an independent state, and had abdicated, a new set of regalia was ordered for the accession of William II to replace the regalia hastily made for his father's proclamation in Brussels. The Crown and Sceptre, nineteenth-century in design, are neither very original nor very precious. They are only made of silver gilt and set with imitation stones and pearls, an unfaithful image of the legendary wealth of the Dutch royal family.

94 Queen Emma. In 1879, William III of Holland, a widower without living heirs, had to marry at sixty-two years of age a twenty-one-year-old German princess, Emma of Waldeck and Pyrmont. A daughter, Wilhelmina, was born a

year later. When William III died in 1890 Queen Emma became regent for her daughter the new Queen Wilhelmina, who was then only ten years old.

95 Queen Wilhelmina was an energetic and authoritarian ruler whose courage during the Second World War rallied all the Dutch around her. Once the War was over she abdicated in favour of her only daughter Juliana. She died in 1962.

96 Queen Juliana, born in 1909, came to the throne in 1948. Like her mother she abdicated (in 1980) in favour of her eldest daughter, Beatrix.

97 Queen Beatrix, born in 1938, has ruled since 1980. In this photograph she is wearing a diadem that was probably a part of the enormous dowry of Anna Pavlovna.

94

95

96

97

Southern Europe: Italy

*I*taly, the largest European warehouse of artistic treasures, is curiously poor in Crown Jewels. The barbarians who underwent civilization while occupying it in the Middle Ages left a few superb pieces. At Monza one can find the remains of the treasure of the kings of Lombardy, including the famous Iron Crown, and at Palermo the pretty crumbs of the treasure of the Norman kings of Sicily. Of the dynasties of patrons of the Renaissance, only the treasure of the greatest, the Medici, remains. Bankers who became *gonfalonieri* (administrators) of the Florentine Republic, and then ruling princes as grand dukes of Tuscany, the Medici were gifted with perfect taste; over the generations they accumulated a marvellous collection of precious objects and also jewels of unequalled refinement. In the eighteenth century their last descendant left the treasure to the city of Florence, where it remains to this day, exhibited at the Pitti Palace.

The Crown Jewels of the Two Sicilies were pawned in the nineteenth century by the last king in order to raise troops to fight Garibaldi. They were never redeemed. The dukes of Savoy had already pawned theirs in Holland, where they were stolen by the French Revolutionary armies and never returned. When they became kings of Italy in 1861 the Savoys did not order a crown or assemble a collection of Crown Jewels. Nevertheless, the three beautiful queens of Italy, Margaret, Helen and Marie José, wore beautiful jewels, which were owned by the last king, Humbert II, who abdicated in 1946 and died in 1983.

On several occasions the Holy See was attacked and occupied and its treasure ransacked, notably by Charles V and Napoleon. All that remains are a few good tiaras from the nineteenth century and a few hideous others given by the faithful to the most recent popes.

98 Crown of Empress Constance. This thirteenth-century jewel is a faithful copy of the crowns of the Byzantine emperors. It was commissioned by Frederick II, who was Holy Roman Emperor through his father and King of Sicily through his mother; it is in the latter capacity that he used this crown.

At twenty-three years of age he married Constance of Aragon, with whom he was deeply in love. When she died four years later the grief-stricken Frederick II placed his own crown in her grave as a pledge of eternal love. It was found there when both their graves were opened in 1781.

99 Crown of Queen Theodolinda
100 The Iron Crown

In the early Middle Ages Northern Italy was an independent kingdom known as Lombardy, ruled by dynasties of invaders from the North. In the sixth century a King of Lombardy married Theodolinda, who was said to be a daughter of the Duke of Bavaria. She brought the Lombards, who had espoused the Arian heresy, back to the Catholic Church. The grateful Pope, Gregory the Great, covered her in gifts, among them the famous Iron Crown. Legend holds that St Helena, after finding the True Cross, gave two nails from it to her son Emperor Constantine the Great. He used one of them as a bit for his horse, and had the other set in a crown of gold, enamel and precious stones; henceforth it was known, in reference to the relic it contains, as the Iron Crown. After vanishing and reappearing several times in the terrible wars that pitted emperors against popes in the Middle Ages, it was brought to Rome in 1452 for the coronation of Emperor Frederick III of Habsburg, and then returned to Bologna for

that of his great-grandson Emperor Charles V. Queen Theodolinda had given it to a convent, along with another crown, of gold, which she had worn; in 1797 this second crown was seized by Napoleon, who had its stones replaced by imitations.

101 Renaissance Pendant in the Shape of a Cock

The dynasty of bankers who ruled Florence, the Medici, produced the greatest collectors Europe has ever seen. They accumulated palaces, villas, paintings, sculptures, tapestries and precious objects in unbelievable profusion. Happily much of it has survived to this day, but almost nothing remains of their collections of jewels and precious stones. This pendant belonged to the last of the Medici, Anna Maria, who married the Elector of Palatine, a German prince of the House of Bavaria, in 1691; it was not returned to Italy from Austria until the Treaty of St Germain in 1919.

102 Ex-voto of Cosimo II

For a long time the Medici were content with being administrators. Then, in the sixteenth century, they secured from Charles V the title of Grand Duke of Tuscany, and it almost seems as if they had exchanged their genius for the honour.

This splendid and theatrical ex-voto of gold and semi-precious stones, typical of the Florentine workshops, was ordered by Grand Duke Cosimo II of Tuscany, to be dedicated to St Charles Borromeo. Cosimo II was the first of the last of the Medici. Their political and financial genius had died out, but the atavism of a patron remained. They continued to commission and collect works of art with passion until the very last.

Three Queens of Italy

103 Margaret of Savoy-Genoa, wife of Humbert I, whom she married in 1868, a brilliant, beautiful, elegant queen.

104 Helen of Montenegro, wife of Victor Emmanuel III, who became King of Italy in 1900; she is remembered as a kind and charitable queen.

105 Marie José of Belgium, wife of the last king, Humbert II. Still in exile from Italy, she has become a historian of renown.

103

104

105

Southern Europe: Spain

This kingdom laden with history, and the only monarchy to have been 'restored' in the twentieth century, has no Crown Jewels.

All that remains from the time of the Visigoth kings of the Middle Ages is the treasure found at Guarrazar, a unique collection of votive crowns, now shared by the Archaeological Museum of Madrid and the Musée de Cluny in Paris. Of the collections of the kings of Castille and Aragon all that remains are a few weapons at the Madrid Armoury and a few nice pieces in Barcelona Cathedral.

Nothing has survived from the treasure of the Habsburg kings of Spain, despite the fabulous riches they accumulated through their colonial empire in South America. Of the Bourbons we have the beautiful objects inherited from the Grand Dauphin of France by his son, Philip V, King of Spain in the eighteenth century. Crown Jewels and princely jewels completely vanished in the nineteenth century between Napoleon's invasion, civil wars and brutal changes of rulers.

For the enthronement of the present king, Juan Carlos I, in 1975, all that could be produced was a miserable symbolic crown, not even of gold, and a sceptre. The royal family has kept only a few jewels from the repeated sales, divisions and thefts. Among them shines the Peregrina, a matchless pearl that belonged in the sixteenth century to Philip II of Spain.

106 **Votive Crown of Recesvinte.** In 1858 a farmer and his wife found an extraordinary treasure in their well, hidden in a hole behind masonry that had been washed away by the rains. The treasure was bought for a song by Isabel II's jeweller. Fearing that he would not get a good price for it in Spain, he smuggled it out of the country and sold it to the French government. The treasure remained at the Musée de Cluny in Paris until 1940, when an agreement – the terms of which remain unknown – was reached between Franco's Spain and Pétain's France. Several pieces, including the Crown of Recesvinte, were brought to Spain, where they have remained ever since. The experts do not agree on whether this crown of gold and precious stones was actually worn by Recesvinte, the last but one of the Visigoth kings of Spain, or whether it was merely a votive crown.

107 Chest with Cameos of the Kings of France

Louis XIV's only legitimate son, the Grand Dauphin, was 'the son of a king, the father of a king, but never king'; he died before his father, but after his second son, his favourite, Philip Duke of Anjou, had become King of Spain as Philip V. At his father's death in 1711 Philip V inherited part of the Grand Dauphin's collections, including this small chest decorated with cameos portraying his ancestors the kings of France and other illustrious Frenchmen.

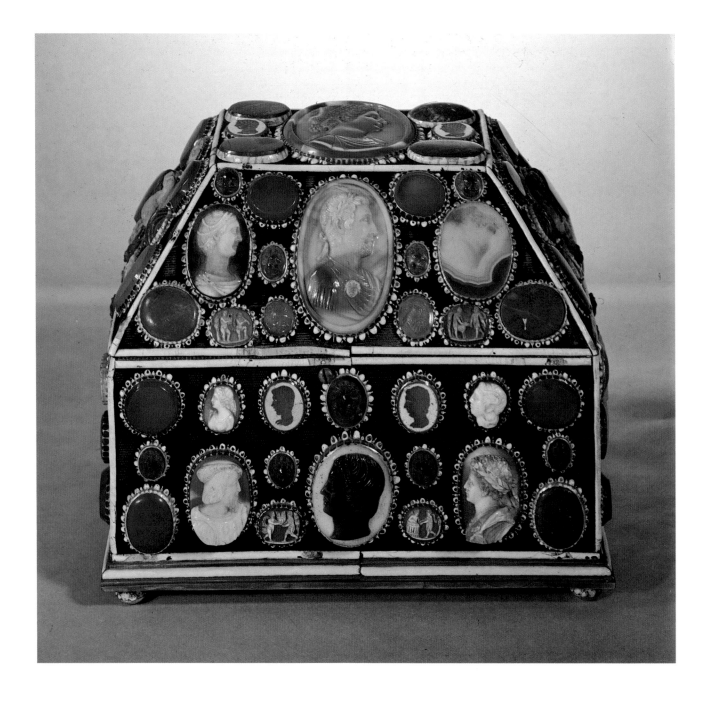

108 Sapphire and Diamond
Necklace of Queen Maria Christina

Maria Christina of Bourbon-Sicily married Ferdinand VII,
King of Spain, the brother of her mother; his first wife had
been the sister of her father. She was twenty-three years old,
he was forty-five and had already been widowed three times.
After she became regent for her daughter Isabella II in 1833,
Maria Christina bravely defended the throne during a long
and terrible civil war. She fell in love with a lowly
bodyguard, Muñoz, bore him many children, made him a
Duke, and finally married him; the scandal forced her to leave
Spain. She had her portrait painted wearing this amazingly
rich necklace. It was sold at Christies in 1982 for $297,000.

Southern Europe: Portugal

*I*n the twelfth century a younger son of the Capetian dynasty of France went to seek his fortune in Iberia. He carved out for himself the County of Portugal and received its title. His son became the first king, and to this day the pretender is his direct descendant. In the Age of Exploration little Portugal seized the lion's share, but she fell into eclipse after the Spanish occupation.

In 1640 an ambitious Spanish woman, married to the younger son of a bastard of the old Royal House of Portugal, expelled her compatriots, restored Portugal to independence, and made her husband John IV. He was called 'The Fortunate' – mostly for having married such a woman. The eighteenth century saw Portugal fall asleep over her immense colonial empire, but in the nineteenth century the occupation by Napoleon's troops and civil war took her fortunes quite low. In 1910 a short revolution brought down the monarchy.

The Crown Jewels in the old Royal Palace of Ajuda form a pretty ensemble. Some important pieces testify to the extraordinary prosperity the kingdom enjoyed in the eighteenth century, and several jewels were added in the nineteenth.

109 **Corsage ornament of diamonds and emeralds.** This enormous brooch, which includes 300 carats of emeralds and 200 of diamonds, is an apt reminder of the fabulous wealth of Portugal in the eighteenth century, built on the gold of its Brazilian colony. It was owned by Queen Marie Anne of Austria, the wife of John V, who was known as 'the king of gold'.

110 **Diamond and ruby brooch of Queen Anne.** This very large brooch inlaid with rubies and diamonds is a perfect example, in size and design, of eighteenth-century jewellery, where the engraving is more important than the quality of the stones. It belonged to Marie Anne of Spain, the wife of Joseph I, whose reign witnessed the greatest natural catastrophe of the century, the Lisbon earthquake.

111 Queen Amelia of France, wife of Charles I, wearing Court dress with the diadem with stars of her mother-in-law Queen Maria Pia of Savoy. In 1908 Queen Amelia was stricken by tragedy when her husband and her eldest son were assassinated before her eyes, shot at point-blank range in their carriage. She managed to save her younger son only by throwing her bouquet at the assassin's head.

112 Diamond Diadem with Stars

This diadem consisting of stars set with large diamonds was commissioned by Queen Maria Pia of Savoy, wife of Louis I, in 1876. A whimsical, spendthrift and stylish queen, she was enormously popular. One day she had a *Te Deum* in Lisbon Cathedral postponed by half-an-hour in order that the sunlight fall through the stained-glass windows at the right angle to catch her red hair at the moment she entered the sanctuary.

113 Miniature of Godoy with Diamonds

It is strange to find, among the Crown Jewels of Portugal, the diamond-set portrait of one of the most scandalous figures of the late eighteenth century. Manuel Godoy, a simple bodyguard, caught the attention of Queen Marie Louise of Spain, Charles VI's wife and Goya's model. Thanks to her he became Duke, Generalissimo, and Knight of the Golden Fleece. The affair was the talk of all the European courts. Perhaps the miniature came to Portugal with the daughter of Queen Marie Louise, Charlotte Joachima, who married John VI of Portugal. She was as unfaithful to him as her mother had been to her husband.

114 Grand Cross of Three Military Orders

This decoration, inlaid with diamonds, rubies and emeralds, was reserved for the use of the reigning king. It combines Portugal's three very ancient military orders: the Order of the Tower and the Sword, founded in the fifteenth century; the Order of St Benedict of Aviz, founded in 1162; and the Order of St James and the Sword, founded in the twelfth century. The jewel dates from the seventeenth century.

Eastern Europe: Hungary

*L*ate in the ninth century the Magyar tribe, cousins to the fearsome Mongols, settled on the rich plains of the Danube under the leadership of their chief Arpad. In 997 his descendant Stephen became the first king of Hungary and, after he had converted to Christianity, her patron saint. After giving Hungary days of glory and greatness the dynasty fell to anarchy, violent deaths and the invasion of Genghis Khan. French princes who ruled Naples inherited Hungary through their wives. National kings followed the French princes, but they were swept aside by the Turkish tidal wave that invaded Hungary and took Budapest. In the meantime the heiress to the French kings of Hungary had married a Bohemian prince of the House of Luxembourg, whose own heiress was to marry the Habsburg Emperor Ferdinand I. The Habsburgs expelled the Turks from Hungary and remained kings there until 1918.

The crown which, according to legend, Pope Sylvester III sent to St Stephen I (in fact it is Byzantine), escaped the Mongols, the Turks, the civil wars and, later, the Nazis and the Soviets. It was sheltered in Canada during the Second World War, and returned to Hungary, with the other instruments of coronation, in 1978. Splendid and unique examples of the art of the goldsmiths of the High Middle Ages, they are exhibited in the National Museum of Budapest.

115 Apostolic Cross. St Stephen I, who Christianized Hungary, was given the title of Apostolic King by Sylvester III. The title was used by all the kings of Hungary, down to the very last, Charles I, Emperor of Austria and King of Hungary. It conferred on the king the right to have carried before him this apostolic cross, a masterpiece of medieval jewellery made of gold and precious stones.

116 Emperor Charles I of Austria and Empress Zita on the day of their coronation as King and Queen of Hungary at Budapest in 1916. Having succeeded his great-uncle Francis Joseph in the midst of the First World War, Charles I wanted to be crowned in Budapest in order to encourage the loyalty of the Hungarians. Due to the circumstances, however, there were neither balls nor banquets, and the King and Queen returned to Vienna on their special train that very evening. Charles I is wearing the Crown of St Stephen, the mantle and the sceptre of the kings of Hungary. Between him and his wife is their eldest son and heir, Archduke Otto.

117 Crown of St Stephen

This crown, supposedly sent to St Stephen I by Pope Sylvester III, became more than an emblem of monarchy. It had its rights, its jurisdiction, its officers, its guard, its land and palace. In 1848, when the revolutionary tides reached Hungary, the population, under the leadership of the poet Louis Kossuth, rose against the Austrians and the oppressive domination of the Habsburgs. But the Russians crushed the revolt. Kossuth ran away with the crown, and buried it under a tree. A traitor sold the information to the Austrians, who extracted the crown and brought it back to the Royal Castle of Buda in great pomp. In its tribulations the crown had slightly suffered, and the cross surmounting it had been twisted. It was never righted, perhaps in order to symbolize the freedom of Hungary.

Béla Kun, the communist who seized power at the end of the First World War, wanted to sell it – or, worse, dismantle it. Luckily he was overthrown before he could carry out his plans. At the end of the Second World War, while the Soviet armies laid siege to Budapest, the crown left in a mysterious special train and was hidden in Austria. Eventually it fell into the hands of the Americans, who locked it up in Fort Knox. It was returned to Hungary only after long negotiations.

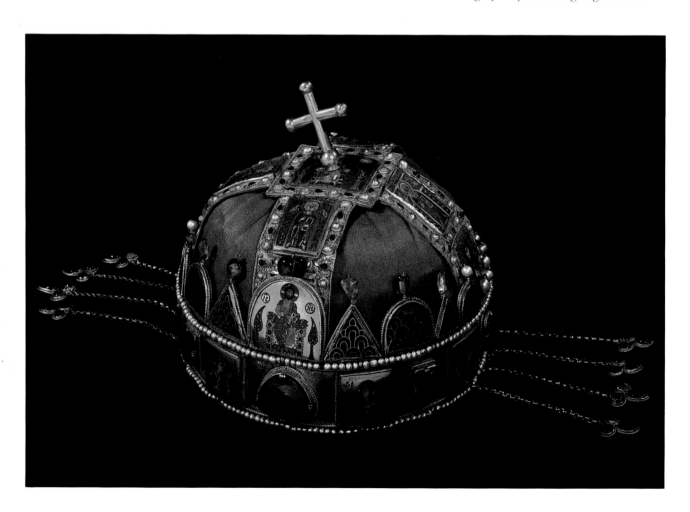

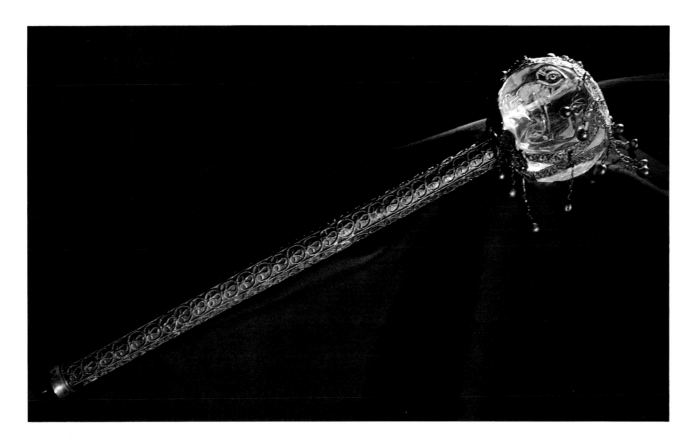

118 Royal Sceptre

The sceptre of Hungary, like its crown, belonged to St Stephen I. Its head is a crystal ball carved with lions. It is thought to be Egyptian; the Muslim craftsmen of the Fatimid Sultans worked with rock crystal, making precious objects that were much appreciated in Europe and often set in the most sacred religious objects of Christendom.

119 Royal Orb

This very simple orb of silver gilt, surmounted by the double cross that is the emblem of Hungary, is adorned with the coat-of-arms of Hungary and the fleur-de-lys of the dynasty under which it was made, the Angevins, in the late fourteenth century. A younger branch of the House of France, the Angevins ruled Naples, inherited Hungary through marriage, and produced several of its greatest rulers.

120 Royal Mantle

The cloth of the Royal Mantle is one of those marvellous silks exported throughout Europe by Byzantium. It was cut by the wife of St Stephen I, Queen Gisella, and presented to a church as a chasuble. Later it became the coronation mantle of the kings. At one time it was sewn together down the front, but Empress Maria Theresa had it opened for her coronation as 'King' of Hungary in 1740. The embroidered figures of St Stephen and Queen Gisella are still visible.

121 Reliquary Brooch of Louis I

The Angevin King of Hungary, Louis I the Great, who came to the throne in 1342, had a particular veneration for the sanctuary of Aix-la-Chapelle (Aachen), to which he sent splendid gifts. One of them was this masterpiece of fourteenth-century jewellery, a reliquary of gold and enamel in the shape of a brooch, decorated with his coat-of-arms. It is still kept there. Although an imported king, Louis I remains one of Hungary's greatest rulers. He restored order, made laws and widened the territory. He was also King of Poland.

Eastern Europe: Bohemia

*I*n the ninth century one of two famous Greek evangelists, St Methodius, travelled to convert pagan Moravia and seized the opportunity to convert the noble Bořivoj, Duke of Bohemia and liegeman of the Přemyslide dynasty. The emperor granted the dynasty the title of King in the eleventh century. In the thirteenth century Ottokar II of Bohemia ruled over vast territories including Hungary and Poland. The dynasty died out and was replaced by the House of Luxembourg in 1310.

The heroic but somewhat impractical John the Blind went off to Crécy in 1346 to die for his French cousins. His son, Charles IV, made of his capital, Prague, a European centre of art and culture. Then the succession became a matter of complicated sleight of hand. The sole heir to Bohemia, Elizabeth, Charles IV's granddaughter, married a Habsburg. Their daughter married a king of Poland. The latter's granddaughter, again a sole heir to Bohemia, brought it to her Habsburg husband, Emperor Ferdinand I, in 1526. From then on the Habsburgs held on to Bohemia. The famous heresy of John Huss in the fifteenth century, largely inspired by anti-German national sentiment, and then the Thirty Years' War in the seventeenth century, showed Bohemia's determination to free herself from her foreign kings. However, she was not to gain independence until 1918, when she assumed the name of Czechoslovakia.

The Jewels of the Bohemian Crown, which are kept in the Cathedral of St Vitus, date back to the fourteenth-century kings of Luxembourg. The pieces are few, but they are remarkably beautiful and interesting.

122 Reliquary Bust of St Ludmilla. In the tenth century the Duchess of Bohemia, Ludmilla, was martyred for her Christian faith. Of course, she was canonized. In the fourteenth century, Charles IV of Luxembourg, King of Bohemia and Roman Emperor, had this bust of silver gilt made to contain her relics. It was kept at the Convent of St George in Prague. A rightful participant, the crowned bust was brought to the Cathedral of St Vitus to witness the coronation of the kings of Bohemia.

123, 124 *Royal Orb and Sceptre*

This sceptre and orb, masterpieces of Renaissance crafts-manship, came from the workshop of Benvenuto Cellini. They were commissioned by Emperor Rudolph II in the late sixteenth century in his capacity as King of Bohemia – he held court at Prague – to replace the instruments of coronation that were far older but much too simple for that splendid sovereign.

125 *Crown of St Wenceslas*

Charles IV of Luxembourg was one of Bohemia's best rulers. He founded the famous University of Prague in 1348, and made of his capital the jewel that it remains to this day. He ordered a very rich crown to adorn the reliquary containing the skull of his predecessor and Bohemia's patron saint, St Wenceslas. This crown was to be removed from the reliquary only for the coronation of the kings of Bohemia. In the cross in the centre is set a relic of the Crown of Thorns. The crown is inlaid with ninety-one gems – emeralds, sapphires, rubies and amethysts – and twenty pearls, and decorated with four large fleurs-de-lys, the emblem of the kings of France. Charles IV had been educated in France, bore the name of the King of France, Charles VI, and had fought for the French at the Battle of Crécy, where his father had lost his life.

Eastern Europe: Poland

*I*n the early eleventh century, under the rule of her first king, Boleslaus I, Poland was an important and a powerful kingdom. By the time of the Renaissance her kings had made of her a brilliant centre of civilization and culture and could well scoff at their neighbours the first tsars.

At the death of the last Jagiellon king in 1572 the Polish monarchy became elective and lost all real power. There were to be a few more moments of greatness, as in the reign of John III Sobieski, Christendom's victor over the Turks in 1683; but Poland's decadence had begun, and her fate was sealed. Her last king, charming Stanislas August Poniatowski, was placed on the throne and then removed, in 1795, by his former mistress Empress Catherine the Great. Poland was partitioned, lost her independence, and fell first in part (in 1795) and then in totality (in 1815) under the Russian yoke, where it has remained, barring a short period between the two world wars, to this day.

Most of the Crown Jewels were removed by the King of Prussia in the late eighteenth century and later destroyed. The remainder disappeared in successive invasions and occupations. All that is left are some superb remains of the treasure of the Jagiellon kings and a few relics from the Middle Ages, including the legendary coronation sword. These objects are now exhibited at Wavel Castle, the old Royal Palace of Cracow, and at the Warsaw Historical Museum.

126 Coronation Sword. This sword – known as 'Szczerbiec' or 'nicked' – with a steel blade and a gold-and-enamel hilt, was made in Lorraine in the thirteenth century. It was originally a sword of justice. The inscription proclaims that it belonged to Duke Boleslaus of Poland. In 1320 it was used in the coronation of King Ladislaus the Short and from then on became the coronation sword of the kings of Poland. When the country was partitioned in 1795, the Austrians received Cracow as their share; but before they could occupy it the Prussians rushed to the city, broke down the gates of Wavel Castle, and carried off all the enormous treasure of the Crown of Poland, including Szczerbiec. They sold the sword, and for many years it passed from hand to hand. In 1886 the Russian Imperial Court bought it in Paris and installed it in the Hermitage Museum in St Petersburg (Leningrad). In 1924 the Soviet Union returned the sword to the once-again – briefly – independent Poland.

127 Orb of Queen Anne Jagiellon

At the death of Sigismund II Augustus in 1572, the Jagiellon dynasty died out and Poland fell into decadence. The Poles chose for their king Henry of Valois; but soon his brother Charles IX died, leaving him the throne of France, and Henry crept away from Wavel Castle under the cover of night – with the diamonds of the Crown. He was succeeded by the sister of Sigismund II Augustus, Anne Jagiellon, and her husband Stephen Bathory, Prince of Transylvania. Queen Anne Jagiellon was passionately fond of jewels; this orb is among the regalia she ordered for her coronation.

128 Fragments of the Chain of Sigismund III

After the death of Stephen Bathory in 1586 the Poles chose for their king the son of the King of Sweden by his Jagiellon wife. Sigismund III Vasa was elected king in 1587. Ruler of an already weakened and impoverished Poland, he nevertheless continued the tradition of patronage begun a century before by a detested Italian woman, Bona Sforza, the wife of Sigismund I. These fragments are from a gold and enamel chain of great refinement, found in the coffin of Sigismund III when it was opened in 1791.

129 Bowl of Sigismund III

Throughout his reign Sigismund III Vasa vainly fought in the midst of endless intrigues to keep both his Swedish and Polish thrones and to reinforce the power of the Polish monarchy against the unruly nobility. It is said that the luckless ruler, an amateur goldsmith, engraved this bowl of gold and enamel, set with large sapphires, himself. Whether he was a remarkable craftsman or was helped, the object remains a perfect testimony to the splendour of the Polish royal treasure, which disappeared after its removal by the Prussians in 1795.

130 Hat of John III Sobieski

Wedged between Orthodox Russia and Protestant Germany, Catholic Poland always enjoyed a particular friendship with the popes, especially after 1683, when John III Sobieski, flying to the rescue of Christendom, crushed the Turks who had encircled Vienna. In gratitude Pope Innocent IX sent him this splendid and strange hat of velvet inlaid with pearls and gold, adorned with a sun and a dove. Later it belonged to Prince Radziwill, who brought it to Russia in 1812. The Soviet Union returned it to Poland in 1924.

131 Coronation Mantle of Tsaritsa Alexandra Feodorovna

After the Congress of Vienna in 1815 Poland became an 'independent' kingdom with a tsar as king, which effectively meant that Russia occupied Poland. Some tsars insisted on maintaining the fiction of the independence and had

themselves crowned as kings of Poland. Thus, in 1829 Tsar Nicholas I was duly crowned in Warsaw. This mantle was worn during the ceremony by his wife, Alexandra Feodorovna, born Princess of Prussia.

132 Crown of Augustus III

Throughout the eighteenth century the history of Poland was one of elections and counter-elections of kings, with furious struggles between the various aspirants to the throne. Each was supported by one or the other of the European powers, which delighted in throwing themselves into the profitable disorder and stoking the fire. Having won the throne in 1734 over his opponent Stanislaus Leczcynski, Frederick Elector of Saxony, as Augustus III of Poland, ordered new instruments of coronation whose richness recalled the legendary splendour of his father, Augustus the Strong, king of Poland before him. The gold crown is set with large diamonds and stones borrowed from the treasure of Saxony.

Russia

*I*n the ninth century a somewhat piratical Viking from Sweden, Rurik, travelled down to Russia and founded a dynasty – certainly a most prolific one, judging by the incalculable number of his descendants. His heirs transformed Kiev into a prosperous state. In the tenth century, one of them, Vladimir I the Great, dazzled by Byzantium, converted to the Greek religion and imposed it on his pagan subjects. He introduced the Byzantine pomp and orthodoxy that were to become the stamp of Russia. His quarrelling descendants founded independent principalities – Moscow, Novgorod, Susdal, Vladimir, all of them renowned centres of icon-painting. The Tartar invaders of the Golden Horde levelled all these princes and vassalized Russia for two centuries.

In the fifteenth century one of Rurik's descendants, Grand Duke of Moscow Ivan III, expelled the Tartars, snapped up all the other principalities ruled by his cousins, and founded the Russian Empire. His grandson Ivan IV the Terrible was the first to adopt the title of Tsar: his death in 1584 sparked a long and dramatic quarrel of succession that lasted until the election in 1613 of the first Romanov, Michael III, an unobtrusive boyar chosen for the throne by his peers. At the dawn of the eighteenth century his grandson Peter the Great made of Russia a world power and opened it to the West. The dynasty died out in 1761 with his daughter, the whimsical Tsaritsa Elizabeth. The Romanov name was perpetuated by the next dynasty, which was in fact of German-Danish origin. It produced a few more great rulers, such as Catherine II the Great, but the mediocrity of the last tsars led to the Revolution of 1917.

The birth of the Russian Empire under Ivan III coincided with the fall of Constantinople, which enabled the tsars to claim inheritance from the Byzantine emperors. They ordered Crown Jewels of an appropriate richness and variety. With the opening to the West the fashion of the Russian Imperial jewels grew more Western, but their abundance and their matchless opulence remained evocative of Oriental splendour. In order to raise desperately needed funds the Soviets disposed of a great part of them in a colossal sale in 1927. Those they kept, however, which are now exhibited in the armoury of the Kremlin, are sufficient testimony to the greatness and durability of the Empire.

133 Crown of Vladimir Monomakh. For his coronation as Tsar in 1547, Ivan the Terrible used this crown of filigreed gold, precious stones and pearls. It might be early fourteenth-century Byzantine. Ivan claimed it had belonged to his distant ancestor Vladimir II Monomakh, the grandson of a Byzantine emperor. Thus he linked young, hesitant Russia to the fabled and holy Byzantine Empire, allowing Moscow to take up the torch of Orthodoxy – and imperialism.

134 Crown of Kazan

In 1552 Ivan the Terrible seized the city of Kazan from the Tartars and put an end to the centuries of humiliating barbarian domination. To commemorate the event he ordered this crown, whose design is strangely reminiscent of the architecture of the Cathedral of St Basil on Red Square in Moscow; it too was built by Ivan IV to celebrate his victories.

Ivan IV became Grand Duke of Russia at the age of three. At eight he saw his mother, the regent, assassinated before his eyes. At thirteen he ordered that a rebel boyar be thrown alive to the wolves. At seventeen he staged his coronation, the first in the history of Russia. Between the victories and defeats that marked his reign, this cruel ruler earned his well-deserved nickname by terrorizing the Empire. He was responsible for innumerable assassinations and atrocious massacres. Nevertheless, through the strange attachment Russians have for their most fearsome rulers, he remained popular.

135 The Orloff Diamond, Imperial Sceptre

In the eighteenth century a deserter from the French Army visited the Temple of Sheringham and noticed the enormous diamond eyes of the Sacred Idol. He pretended to be an ardent convert to Hinduism and begged to be allowed to spend the night in the temple, in order to 'better pray to Brahma'. He then prised out one of the idol's eyes and absconded with it. In London he sold it to a Jewish merchant, and soon afterwards it was offered to Empress Catherine the Great of Russia, who refused, thinking the price excessive. Thereupon it was bought by her former lover, Prince Gregory Orloff, for the sum of ninety thousand pounds. As a simple soldier years before, Orloff had become Catherine's lover, helped her seize power through a *coup d'état*, and with his own hands killed her husband Peter III who had become, under the circumstances, something of an embarrassment. Then he fell into disgrace and was sent into exile. Ever since he had sought a way of recovering Catherine's favour, and now he bought the diamond and gave it to her. She accepted, but did not recall him. He died insane not long afterwards, still exiled on his estates. Catherine never wore the 200-carat diamond, but had it set in the sceptre fashioned for her coronation.

136 Throne of Boris Godunov

Relations between Russia and Persia have always been close, for the northern Empire always felt a highly imperialistic affection for the Asiatic Empire of the south. In the early seventeenth century, when it was Russia who was weak and Persia strong, Shah Abbas, one of the greatest Persian rulers, sent this gold-covered wood throne inlaid with rubies and turquoise to Tsar Boris Godunov. He sat on it at his coronation, but did not enjoy it long. Soon after, in 1603, came a pretender who claimed to be Dimitry, the assassinated son of Ivan the Terrible, and who led the people in a rebellion against Boris Godunov. In 1605 Godunov died alone, abandoned. The fake Dimitry entered Moscow and had himself crowned on Shah Abbas's throne; but soon the boyars realized that with Dimitry they had let the hated Poles into Russia, and assassinated him.

137 Emerald engraved with the portrait of Catherine II the Great

Prince Orloff gave Catherine the Great the diamond that bears his name. She in turn gave him, among other luxurious presents, this 19.40-carat emerald engraved with her profile and surrounded by diamonds. The engraving is a considerable achievement, for emerald is a brittle stone that can break under the slightest incision. This gem has a twin, also engraved with the great Empress's profile, which is still in the Kremlin.

138 Diamond Brooch

Empress Catherine the Great never forgot that she had once been a very impoverished German princess. When she found herself ruling the immense Russian Empire, she enjoyed spending, and endlessly commissioned jewels – not the heavy Asiatic-fashioned jewels of ancient tsars but light, elegant jewels in the style of eighteenth-century France, like this one.

139 Nuptial Crown

Hastily fashioned in the mid-nineteenth century from pieces of a diamond belt – that had belonged to Catherine the Great – sewn on to red velvet, this crown was worn by all the brides of the Russian Imperial family on their wedding day. Sold by the Soviets after the 1917 Revolution, it passed from hand to hand before coming into the possession of Mrs Merriweather Post, the famous American billionairess and collector.

140 Pearl and Diamond Diadem

This pearl and diamond diadem of bold and elegant design was part of the innumerable beautiful jewels of the Russian Crown, which were at the disposal of the Imperial family. Like so many others it was sold for a song in one of the colossal sales organized by the Soviets in the 1920s. Later it came into the possession of an American, Gladys Deacon, who married the ninth Duke of Marlborough.

141 Pearl and Diamond Necklace

This jewel belonged to Empress Maria Feodorovna, the mother of Nicholas II. Taken by surprise at the Revolution, she was able to escape only with her 'small', 'everyday' jewels, including this one, which gives an indication of the richness of the 'evening' parures she was forced to leave behind. At her death the pendant was inherited by her daughter Grand Duchess Xenia, like her one of the few members of the Imperial family to survive the Revolution.

142 Empress Maria Feodorovna, born Dagmar of Denmark, was the wife of Alexander III and mother of Nicholas II. She survived the Revolution, refusing to believe in the massacre of her son and family. In this photograph she is wearing Court dress with one of the most precious jewels of the Russian treasure, a necklace of thirty-six enormous diamonds weighing a total of 475 carats; the centre one alone weighs 32 carats.

143 Nicholas II and Alexandra Feodorovna in fancy dress. In 1903 the Russian Court staged at the Hermitage in St Petersburg (Leningrad) an extraordinary masked ball on the theme of seventeenth-century Russia. The last Tsar and his wife are dressed in period costumes embroidered with gems from the Crown Jewels. Tsaritsa Alexandra is wearing a necklace made especially for the occasion by Fabergé, in diamonds and sapphires, including one enormous 159-carat cabochon sapphire.

Picture Sources and Acknowledgments

Photographic material supplied by the museums and collections unless otherwise stated

Frontispiece Imperial Eagle (*h* 8.3 cm, $3\frac{1}{3}$ in.) Apollon Gallery, Louvre, Paris. Photo Claus Hansmann.

2 Reliquary Bust of Charlemagne (*h* 86.3 cm, 34 in.) Cathedral Treasure, Aix-La-Chapelle. Photo Bavaria Verlag.

3 Talisman of Charlemagne (*l* 7.3 cm, $2\frac{7}{8}$ in.) Palais de Tau, Reims. Photo Arch. Phot. Paris. SPADEM.

4 Imperial Cross (*h* 77 cm, $30\frac{5}{8}$ in.) Kunsthistorisches Museum, Vienna. Photo Meyer.

5 Crown of Empress Kunigunde (*d* 19 cm, $7\frac{1}{2}$ in.) Treasury Room, Palace of the Residenz, Munich. Photo Claus Hansmann.

6 The Peregrina Pearl. Private collection.

7 Decoration of the Golden Fleece (*w* 12.5 cm, $4\frac{7}{8}$ in.) Ajuda Palace, Lisbon.

8 The Goslar Reliquary. National History Museum, Stockholm.

9 The Phoenix Jewel of Elizabeth I (*w* 4.6 cm, $1\frac{7}{8}$ in.) British Museum, London.

10 Silver Baptismal Font. Royal Palace, Stockholm. Photo Claus Hansmann.

11 Victoria Eugenia, granddaughter of Queen Victoria. Photo private collection.

12 Elizabeth II at her coronation. Photo John Topham Picture Library.

13 Imperial Orb (*h* 21 cm, $8\frac{1}{4}$ in.) Kunsthistorisches Museum, Vienna. Photo Bavaria Verlag.

14 Crown of Charlemagne (*h* at front 15.6 cm, $6\frac{1}{8}$ in.) Kunsthistorisches Museum, Vienna. Photo Meyer.

15 Imperial Mantle (*w* 342 cm, 136 in.) Kunsthistorisches Museum, Vienna. Photo Meyer.

16 Imperial Shoes (*l* 25.5 and 26 cm, 10 and $10\frac{1}{8}$ in.) Kunsthistorisches Museum, Vienna. Photo Meyer.

17 Crown of Emperor Rudolph II (*h* 28.6 cm, $11\frac{1}{4}$ in.) Kunsthistorisches Museum, Vienna. Photo Meyer.

18 Imperial Sceptre of Austria (*l* 75.5 cm, $29\frac{3}{4}$ in.) Kunsthistorisches Museum, Vienna. Photo Meyer.

19 Amethyst of Charles II. Kunsthistorisches Museum, Vienna. Photo Meyer.

20 La Bella. Kunsthistorisches Museum, Vienna. Photo Meyer.

21 Cameo of Noah (*l* 5.3 cm, $2\frac{1}{8}$ in.) British Museum, London.

22 Elizabeth of Bavaria. Photo Keystone Press Agency Ltd.

23 Zita of Bourbon-Parme, wife of Charles I of Austria. Photo Bildarchiv Preussischer Kulturbesitz.

24 Brooch in the shape of a trophy (*l* 17 cm, $6\frac{3}{4}$ in.) Residenz Palace, Munich. Photo Claus Hansmann.

25 Orb of the Kings of Bavaria (*d* 12 cm, $4\frac{3}{4}$ in.) Residenz Palace, Munich. Photo Claus Hansmann.

26 Crown of Princess Blanche. Residenz Palace, Munich. Photo Bavaria Verlag.

27 Diadem and Bracelets of Queen Theresa. Residenz Palace, Munich. Photo Claus Hansmann.

28 The Palatinate Pearl (5 × 8 cm, 2 × $3\frac{1}{8}$ in.) Residenz Palace, Munich. Photo Claus Hansmann.

29 Hat-brooch of Ludwig II (7 × 4 cm, $2\frac{3}{4}$ × $1\frac{1}{2}$ in.) Residenz Palace, Munich. Photo Claus Hansmann.

30 Crown of the Queens of Bavaria (*h* & *d* 17 cm, $6\frac{3}{4}$ in.) Residenz Palace, Munich. Photo Claus Hansmann.

31 Ludwig III of Bavaria. Photo Bilderdienst Süddeutscher Verlag.

32 The Court of Auranzeb. Green Vault, Dresden. Photo Claus Hansmann.

33 Pendant with Coats-of-Arms (*h* 12.2 cm, $4\frac{3}{4}$ in.) Green Vault, Dresden. Photo Claus Hansmann.

34 Sword of Augustus the Strong. Green Vault, Dresden. Photo Claus Hansmann.

35 The Green Diamond of Dresden. Green Vault, Dresden. Photo Claus Hansmann.

36 Emerald Order of the White Eagle. Green Vault, Dresden. Photo Claus Hansmann.

37 Royal Sceptre of Prussia. Charlottenburg Palace, Berlin.

38 Snuffbox of Frederick the Great (*w* 10.4 cm, $4\frac{1}{8}$ in.) Photo Christie's, Geneva.

39 Royal Crown of Prussia. Hohenzollern Castle. Photo Hero Bild.

40 Emperor William I. Photo BBC Hulton Picture Library.

41 The coronation of William I. Photo Bildarchiv Preussischer Kulturbesitz.

42 Statue of Charles VI (*h* 62 cm, 24 in.) Photo Edimedia.

43 Hand of Justice (39 cm, 15 in.) Apollon Gallery, Louvre, Paris. Photo Réunion des Musées Nationaux.

44 Order of St Michael *(actual size)*. Monseigneur Le Comte de Paris. Photo Brumaire.

45 Parure of sapphires and diamonds of Queen Marie Antoinette. Monseigneur le Comte de Paris. Photo Brumaire.

46 The Duchess of Guise. Photo private collection.

47 The Countess of Paris. Photo private collection.

48 The Regent Diamond. Apollon Gallery, Louvre, Paris. Photo Réunion des Musées Nationaux.

49 Diadem of Emeralds and Diamonds. Photo Wartski, London.

50 The Sancy Diamond. Apollon Gallery, Louvre, Paris. Photo Réunion des Musées Nationaux.

51 The Mancini Pearls. Photo Christie's, New York.

52 Clasp of St Louis. Apollon Gallery, Louvre, Paris. Photo Réunion des Musées Nationaux.

53 Joyeuse, the sword of Charlemagne. Apollon Gallery, Louvre, Paris. Photo Claus Hansmann.

54 Sword of Charles X. Formerly Apollon Gallery, Louvre, Paris. Photo Réunion des Musées Nationaux.

55 Necklace made with the diamonds of the Queen's necklace. Private collection, London.

56 Model of the Queen's necklace. Photo Zalewski.

57 The Hope Diamond. Smithsonian Institution, Washington D.C.

58, 59 Imperial State Crown. Tower of London. Crown copyright. Photo H.M.S.O.

60 King Alfred's Jewel (*l* 6.2 cm, $2\frac{3}{8}$ in.) Ashmolean Museum, Oxford.

61 Coronation Throne. Westminster Abbey, London. Photo by courtesy of the Dean and Chapter of Westminster.

62 The King's Sceptre with the Cross; The King's Sceptre with the Dove; The Queen's Sceptre with the Cross; The Queen's Ivory Road. Tower of London. Crown copyright. Photo H.M.S.O.

63 The Pendant of Naseby (*l* 9 cm, $3\frac{1}{2}$ in.) Sir John Soane's Museum, London. Photo Trustees of the Sir John Soane's Museum.

64 Small Diamond Crown of Queen Victoria. Tower of London. Crown copyright. Photo H.M.S.O.

65 Queen Victoria. Photo private collection.

66 Indian Armlet with replica of the Koh-i-Noor Diamond. Photo H.M.S.O.

67 Queen Alexandra. Photo private collection.

68 Crown of Queen Elizabeth the Queen Mother. Tower of London. Photo H.M.S.O.

69 St Edward's Crown. Tower of London. Crown copyright. Photo H.M.S.O.

70 The Darnley Jewel (*h* 12.5 cm, 5 in.) Reproduced by Gracious Permission of Her Majesty the Queen.

71 Royal Crown of Scotland. Edinburgh Castle. Reproduced by permission of the Controller of Her Majesty's Stationery Office. Photo H.M.S.O. Edinburgh.

72 Elizabeth II. Photo John Topham Picture Library.

73 Ruby Ring of Charles I. Edinburgh Castle. Reproduced by permission of the Controller of Her Majesty's Stationery Office. Photo H.M.S.O. Edinburgh.

74 Sword of Gustavus III. The Treasury, Royal Palace, Stockholm.

75 Silver Throne. Royal Palace, Stockholm. Photo Claus Hansmann.

76 Crown of Queen Maria Eleonora. The Treasury, Royal Palace, Stockholm.

77 Crown of the Hereditary Prince. The Treasury, Royal Palace, Stockholm.

78, 79 Orb and Crown of Eric XIV. The Treasury, Royal Palace, Stockholm.

80 Louise of Battenberg. Photo Popperfoto.

81 Gustavus V. Photo Royal Collection, Stockholm.

82 King's crown, sword, orb, sceptre and ampulla *(actual size)*. Photo Mittet Foto.

83 Haakon VII and Queen Maud. Reproduced by Gracious Permission of Her Majesty The Queen.

84 Royal Throne with Unicorns. Rosenborg Castle, Copenhagen.

85 Crown of Christian IV. Rosenborg Castle, Copenhagen. Photo Claus Hansmann.

86 Order of the Elephant (*h* 5.6 cm, $2\frac{1}{4}$ in.) Rosenborg Castle, Copenhagen. Photo Claus Hansmann.

87 Ampulla. Rosenborg Castle, Copenhagen.

88 Sceptre of Frederick III. Rosenborg Castle, Copenhagen.

89 Bracelet, Necklace and Brooch of Diamonds, Rubies and Pearls. Rosenborg Castle, Copenhagen.

90 Ingrid of Sweden. Photo Keystone Press Agency.

91 Margaret II, Queen of Denmark. Photo Keystone Press Agency.

92 Orb and Sword of William II. Royal Palace, The Hague. Photo Netherlands Information Service.

93 Crown and Sceptre of William II. Royal Palace, The Hague. Photo Netherlands Information Service.

94 Queen Emma. Photo Netherlands Information Service.

95 Queen Wilhelmina. Photo Popperfoto.

96 Queen Juliana. Photo Netherlands Information Service.

97 Queen Beatrix. Photo Netherlands Information Service.

98 Crown of Empress Constance. Treasury of the Cathedral of Palermo. Photo Scala.

99 Crown of Queen Theodolinda. Treasury of the Cathedral of Monza. Photo Scala.

100 Iron Crown. Treasury of the Cathedral of Monza. Photo Scala.

101 Renaissance Pendant in the Shape of a Cock. Museo degli Argenti, Palazzo Pitti, Florence. Photo Scala.

102 Ex-voto of Cosimo II. Museo degli Argenti, Palazzo Pitti, Florence. Photo Scala.

103 Margaret of Savoy-Genoa. Photo Popperfoto.

104 Helen of Montenegro. Photo Popperfoto.

105 Marie-José of Belgium. Photo BBC Hulton Picture Library.

106 Votive Crown of Recesvinte. Archaeological Museum, Madrid. Photo Oronoz.

107 Chest with Cameos of the Kings of France (12.5 × 15.7 × 12.3 cm, $4\frac{7}{8}$ × $6\frac{1}{4}$ × $4\frac{3}{4}$ in.) Treasure of the Dauphin, Prado, Madrid. Photo Claus Hansmann.

108 Sapphire and Diamond

Necklace of Queen Maria Christina. Photo Sotheby Parke Bernet/Editorial Photocolor Archive Inc.

109 Corsage ornament of diamonds and emeralds (*w* 19cm, 7¼ in.) Palace of Ajuda, Lisbon.

110 Diamond and ruby brooch of Queen Anne. Photo Christie's, Geneva.

111 Queen Amelia of France. Photo private collection.

112 Diamond Diadem with Stars. Palace of Ajuda, Lisbon.

113 Miniature of Godoy with Diamonds. Palace of Ajuda, Lisbon.

114 Grand Cross of Three Military Orders (*h* 15cm, 5⅞ in.) Palace of Ajuda, Lisbon.

115 Apostolic Cross. Treasury of the Cathedral of Gran, Hungary. Photo Corvina Press.

116 Emperor Charles I and Empress Zita. Photo Popperfoto.

117 Crown of St Stephen. National Museum, Budapest. Photo Interfoto MTI.

118 Royal Sceptre. National Museum, Budapest. Photo Interfoto MTI.

119 Royal Orb. National Museum, Budapest.

120 Royal Mantle. National Museum, Budapest.

121 Reliquary Brooch of Louis I. Aix-la-Chapelle, Treasury of the Cathedral. Photo Ann Münchow.

122 Reliquary Bust of St Ludmilla. Cathedral of St Vitus, Prague. Photo Karel Neubert.

123, 124 Royal Orb and Sceptre. Cathedral of St Vitus, Prague. Photo Karel Neubert.

125 Crown of St Wenceslas. Cathedral of St Vitus, Prague. Photo Karel Neubert.

126 Coronation Sword. Wavel Castle, Cracow. Photo Lukasz Schuster/Wavel State Collections of Art.

127 Orb of Queen Anne Jagiellon. Wavel Castle, Cracow. Photo Lukasz Schuster/Wavel State Collections of Art.

128 Fragments of the chain of Sigismund III. Wavel Castle, Cracow. Photo Lukasz Schuster/Wavel State Collections of Art.

129 Bowl of Sigismund III. Residenz Palace, Munich (7.5 × 17.7 cm, 2⅜ × 6¾ in.) Photo Claus Hansmann.

130 Hat of John III Sobieski. Wavel Castle, Cracow. Photo Lukasz Schuster/Wavel State Collections of Art.

131 Coronation Mantle of Tsarita Alexandra Feodorovna. National Museum, Warsaw. Photo Teresa Zótowska.

132 Crown of Augustus III. National Museum, Warsaw. Photo Teresa Zótowska.

133 Crown of Vladimir Monomakh. Armoury, Kremlin, Moscow. Photo Claus Hansmann.

134 Crown of Kazan. Armoury, Kremlin, Moscow. Photo Novosti Press Agency.

135 The Orloff Diamond, Imperial Sceptre. Armoury, Kremlin, Moscow. Photo Novosti Press Agency.

136 Throne of Boris Godunov. Armoury, Kremlin, Moscow. Photo Claus Hansmann.

137 Emerald engraved with the portrait of Catherine II the Great. Photo Christie's, Geneva.

138 Diamond Brooch. Courtesy S. J. Phillips, London.

139 Nuptial Crown. National Museum of Natural History, Smithsonian Institution, Washington D.C, Photo Lee Boltin.

140 Pearl and Diamond Diadem. Photo Christie's, London.

141 Pearl and Diamond Necklace. Photo Christie's, Geneva.

142 Empress Maria Feodorovna. Photo Keystone Press Agency.

143 Nicholas II and Alexandra Feodorovna. Photo BBC Hulton Picture Library.

Index